THE REFERENCE S

Volume XIII

No.

5. **Public Housing in America.** M. B. Schnapper. $1.25.
6. **United States Foreign Policy (Supplement)** J. E. Johnsen. 75c.
7. **Student Congress Movement: with Discussion on American Neutrality.** L. S. Judson. $1.25.
8. **The Railroads: Government Ownership in Practice (Supplement to The Railroad Problem)** H. B. Summers and R. E. Summers. 25c.
9. **The National Labor Relations Act. Should It Be Amended?** J. E. Johnsen. $1.25.
10. **Trade Unions and the Anti-Trust Laws.** J. E. Johnsen. $1.25.

Volume XII. $6

No.

1. **Anglo-American Agreement.** H. B. Summers. 25c.
2. **Discussion Methods Explained and Illustrated.** J. V. Garland and C. F. Phillips. (rev. ed. 1940) $1.25.
3. **The State Sales Tax.** E. R. Nichols and others. 25c.
4. **Dictatorships vs. Democracies. 1938 (Supplement to Anglo-American Agreements)** H. B. Summers and R. E. Summers. 75c.
5. **Pump-priming Theory of Government Spending.** E. R. Nichols and William E. Roskam. 25c.
6. **United States Foreign Policy: Isolation or Alliance.** J. E. Johnsen. 25c.
7. **Chain Stores and Legislation.** Daniel Bloomfield. $1.25.
8. **The United States and War.** J. E. Johnsen. 90c.
9. **Debate Index.** E. M. Phelps. 75c.
10. **Radio Censorship.** H. B. Summers. $1.25.

Volume XI. $6

No.

1. **Unicameral Legislatures.** H. B. Summers. 90c.
2. **Consumers' Cooperatives.** J. E. Johnsen, J. V. Garland, C. F. Phillips. 90c.
3. **Industrial versus Craft Unionism.** J. E. Johnsen. 90c.
4. **Reorganization of the Supreme Court.** J. E. Johnsen. 90c.
5. **Unicameralism in Practice: The Nebraska Legislative System.** H. B. Summers. 90c.
6. **Modern Group Discussion.** L. and E. Judson. 90c.
7. **Arbitration and the National Labor Relations Board.** E. R. Nichols and J. W. Logan. 90c.
8. **Peace and Rearmament.** J. E. Johnsen. 20c.
9. **Chinese-Japanese War, 1937-.** J. E. Johnsen. 90c.
10. **Representative American Speeches: 1937-1938.** A. C. Baird. $1.25.

Volume X. $4.20

No.

1. **Collective Bargaining.** J. E. Johnsen. 90c.
2. **Lotteries.** H. M. Muller. 90c.
3. **Old Age Pensions.** J. E. Johnsen. 90c.

5. **Socialization of Medicine.** J. E. Johnsen. 90c.
6. **Limitation of Power of Supreme Court to Declare Acts of Congress Unconstitutional.** J. E. Johnsen. 90c.
9. **Government Ownership of Electric Utilities.** J. E. Johnsen. 90c.
10. **The Crisis in the Electric Utilities.** Garland and Phillips. 20c.

THE REFERENCE SHELF

Vol. 16 No. 4

WAGE STABILIZATION AND INFLATION

Compiled by

JULIA E. JOHNSEN

NEW YORK
THE H. W. WILSON COMPANY
1943

Published May 1943

PRINTED IN THE UNITED STATES OF AMERICA

PREFACE

Among the various remedies proposed for inflationary control that of wage stabilization has received considerable attention. Closely linked to price control and held by many to be an essential concomitant to the success of such a measure, wage ceilings became somewhat tardily a part of the governmental anti-inflationary program. Expediency, concern for labor, an expectation that price control might itself provide an indirect measure of wage control, these and other considerations tended to defer the early implementing of efforts to control the inflationary spiral with a definite and firm governmental policy toward labor.

Notwithstanding the Emergency Price Control Act of January 1942, the early remedies adopted for inflation proved increasingly inadequate both as to prices and wages. The National War Labor Board had, by July 1942, developed its Little Steel formula under which, together with its considerations of substandard wages and other wage inequities, a steady rise in wage levels was in process. Thousands of wage cases were brought before the Board. Meanwhile, in his message to Congress on April 27th, the President set forth a seven-point anti-inflationary program, repeated in his message of September 7th, in which he included a request for more rigid controls over wages. This was implemented on October 3rd by his establishment of the Office of Economic Stabilization under the direction of James F. Brynes, to whom wide authority over economic matters was accorded, including prices, wages and salaries. In a late executive order, given April 8th of the present year, the President once more, in no uncertain tones, gave expression to a definite "hold-the-line" order for wages.

Wage stabilization presents a multitude of factors to perplex labor, industry, government and the public alike. It is more than an economic measure presented against the background of a successful prosecution of the war, and a controversial question as to the relation of wages to inflation, and the adequacy of other anti-inflationary controls without the addition of wage regulation.

In the larger view, wage stabilization touches upon far-reaching problems of social and economic import and, in ultimate effects, upon postwar adjustments and national welfare as well. Since the latest Presidential order labor has continued to press demands for a "realistic" consideration of wages; the $2 a day demand of the United Mine Workers of America was met by a suggested substitute of a guaranteed annual wage, a suggestion heralded as exceeding the original demand and as a camouflaged wage rise that would inevitably start a new spiral of wage demands on the part of labor.

This number of the Reference Shelf is supplementary to that entitled *Wages and Prices* compiled by Robert E. Summers and published in April, 1942. It includes, in bibliography and discussions, new materials to date, covering a period when the subject has taken on new immediacy and become of increasing vital concern.

The compiler gratefully acknowledges various courtesies, including copyright permissions, which have facilitated and made possible the preparation of this book.

JULIA E. JOHNSEN

April 20, 1943

CONTENTS

GENERAL DISCUSSION

STABILIZING THE COST OF LIVING [1]

Four months ago, on April 27, 1942, I laid before the Congress a seven-point national economic policy designed to stabilize the domestic economy of the United States for the period of the war. The objective of that program was to prevent any substantial further rise in the cost of living.

It is not necessary for me to enumerate again the disastrous results of a runaway cost of living—disastrous to all of us, farmers, laborers, businessmen—the nation itself. When the cost of living spirals upward, everybody becomes poorer, because the money he has and the money he earns buys so much less. At the same time the cost of war, paid ultimately from taxes of the people, is needlessly increased by many billions of dollars. The national debt, at the end of the war, would become unnecessarily greater. Indeed, the prevention of a spiraling domestic economy is a vital part of the winning of the war itself.

I reiterate the seven-point program which I presented April 27, 1942:

1. To keep the cost of living from spiraling upward, we must tax heavily, and in that process keep personal and corporate profits at a reasonable rate, the word "reasonable" being defined at a low level.

2. To keep the cost of living from spiraling upward, we must fix ceilings on the prices which consumers, retailers, wholesalers, and manufacturers pay for the things they buy; and ceilings on rents for dwellings in all areas affected by war industries.

3. To keep the cost of living from spiraling upward, we must stabilize the remuneration received by individuals for their work.

[1] By President Franklin D. Roosevelt. From Message to Congress, September 7, 1942. *Congressional Record*. 88:7283-4. September 7, 1942.

4. To keep the cost of living from spiraling upward, we must stabilize the prices received by growers for the products of their lands.

5. To keep the cost of living from spiraling upward, we must encourage all citizens to contribute to the cost of winning this war by purchasing war bonds with their earnings instead of using those earnings to buy articles which are not essential.

6. To keep the cost of living from spiraling upward, we must ration all essential commodities of which there is a scarcity, so that they may be distributed fairly among consumers and not merely in accordance with financial ability to pay high prices for them.

7. To keep the cost of living from spiraling upward, we must discourage credit and installment buying, and encourage the paying off of debts, mortgages, and other obligations; for this promotes savings, retards excessive buying, and adds to the amount available to the creditors for the purchase of war bonds.

In my message of four months ago, I pointed out that in order to succeed in our objective of stabilization it was necessary to move on all seven fronts at the same time; but that two of them called for legislation by the Congress before action could be taken. It was obvious then, and it is obvious now, that unless those two are realized, the whole objective must fail. These are points numbered 1 and 4—namely, an adequate tax program and a law permitting the fixing of price ceilings on farm products at parity prices.

I regret to have to call to your attention the fact that neither of these two essential pieces of legislation has as yet been enacted into law. That delay has now reached the point of danger to our whole economy.

However, we are carrying out, by Executive action, the other parts of the seven-point program which did not require congressional action.

Price ceilings have been fixed on practically all commodities (other than certain exempted agricultural products), and on rents in war-production areas of the United States.

This process of keeping prices and rents at reasonable levels, constitutes one of the most far-reaching economic steps that this nation has ever taken—in time of peace or war.

Our experience during the last four months has proved that general control of prices is possible—but only if that control is all inclusive. If, however, the costs of production, including labor, are left free to rise indiscriminately, or if other major elements in the costs of living are left unregulated, price control becomes impossible. If markets are flooded with purchasing power in excess of available goods, without taking adequate measures to siphon off the excess purchasing power, price control becomes likewise impossible.

Our entire effort to hold the cost of living at its present level is now being sapped and undermined by further increases in farm prices and in wages, and by an ever-continuing pressure on prices resulting from the rising purchasing power of our people.

Annual wage and salary disbursements have increased from 43.7 billion dollars in 1939 to an estimated 75 billion dollars in 1942. This represents an increase of 71 per cent. To obtain a full appreciation of what that increase means, we should remember that 75 billion dollars is more than our total national income was during any single year in the 1930's. Due to constantly increasing employment, overtime, and wage-rate increases, the annual wage and salary bill for the entire country has been rising by more than a billion dollars a month.

It is impossible for the cost of living to be stabilized while farm prices continue to rise. You cannot expect the laborer to maintain a fixed wage level if everything he wears and eats begins to go up drastically in price. On the other hand, it is impossible to keep any prices stable—farm prices or other prices—if wage rates, one of the most important elements in the cost of production, continue to increase.

But even if the process of stabilization of all prices and wages at present levels were to be brought about, there would still remain the great upward pressure on the cost of living created by the vast amount of purchasing power which has been earned in all sections of the country. The national income has been increasing since January 1, 1941, at the average rate of 2 per cent each month. This purchasing power now exceeds by an estimated 20 billions the amount of goods which will be available for purchase by civilians this year. The result obviously is that people compete more and more for the available supply of goods; and the pressure of this great demand compared with the small supply—which will become smaller and smaller—continually threatens to disrupt our whole price structure.

A recent study by the Bureau of Labor Statistics has shown very strikingly how much the incomes of the average of families have gone up during the first quarter of 1942. If we assume that the income for the first quarter of 1942 is a fair basis for estimating what the family income will be for the entire year, the results of the study show that whereas less than one-fourth of all families in the United States received as much as $2,500 in 1941, more than one-third will have $2,500 or more in 1942. This shows how much the purchasing power of the average American family has gone up as a result of war production and how essential it is to control that purchasing power by taxation and by investment in war bonds.

We also know that as the war goes on there will not be an adequate supply of all civilian goods; that only through strict rationing, wherever necessary, will these goods be equitably distributed. We are determined that no group shall suffer a shrinkage of its normal quota of basic necessities because some richer group can buy all the available supply at high prices.

In normal peacetimes the ordinary processes of collective bargaining are sufficient in themselves. But in wartimes and particularly in times of greatly increasing prices, the government itself has a very vital interest in seeing to it that wages are kept in balance with the rest of the economy. It is still the policy of the federal government to encourage free collective bargaining between employers and workers; and that policy will continue. Owing to the fact that costs of production are now, in so many cases, being passed on to the government, and that so large a percentage of profits would be taken away by taxation, collective bargaining between employers and employees has changed a great deal from what it was in peacetimes. In times of danger to our economy the government itself must step into the situation to see to it that the processes of collective bargaining and arbitration and conciliation are not permitted to break up the balances between the different economic factors in our system.

War calls for sacrifice. War makes sacrifice a privilege. That sacrifice will have to be expressed in terms of a lack of many of the things to which we all have become accustomed. Workers, farmers, white-collar people, and businessmen must expect that. No one can expect that, during the war, he will always be able to buy what he can buy today.

If we are to keep wages effectively stabilized, it becomes imperative, in fairness to the worker, to keep equally stable the cost of food and clothing and shelter and other articles used by workers.

Prices and rents should not be allowed to advance so drastically ahead of wage rates that the real wage of workers as of today—their ability to buy food and clothing and medical care—will be cut down. For if the cost of living goes up as fast as it is threatening to do in the immediate future, it will be unjust, in fact impossible, to deny workers rises in wages which would meet at least a part of that increase.

The cost of all food used by wage earners—controlled and uncontrolled—has been going up at the rate of 1¼ per cent per month since the price ceilings were set in May 1942. If this rise should be permitted to continue, the increased cost of food to wage earners next May would be more than 15 per cent over the level which existed when the ceilings were set.

This would be equal to imposing a 15 per cent sales tax on all food purchased by wage earners. Obviously no one would consider imposing such a tax.

This drastic increase has been caused, and will be caused, chiefly by the fact that a number of food commodities are exempt under existing law.

In the case of these exempt commodities the increases are even more startling. The cost of such food used by wage earners has been rising at an average of 3¼ per cent per month since May 1, 1942.

Prices received by farmers have risen 85 per cent since the outbreak of the war in September 1939, and these prices are continuing to rise. Cash farm income including government payments, has increased from 8.7 billion dollars in 1939 to substantially more than 15 billion dollars in 1942. This is an increase of about 75 per cent.

The movement of uncontrolled food prices since May 18, 1942, the date when price regulation became effective, has been so drastic as to constitute an immediate threat to the whole price structure, to the entire cost of living, and to any attempt to stabilize wages.

Within two months after the date that price regulation became effective, the prices of controlled foods actually fell seven-tenths of 1 per cent. But uncontrolled foods advanced 7.3 per cent during the same period, and are still going up. . . .

If wages should be stabilized and farm prices be permitted to rise at anything like the present rate, workers will have to bear the major part of the increase. This we cannot ask. The Congress must realize that unless the existing control over farm prices is strengthened, we must abandon our efforts to stabilize wages and salaries and the cost of living. If that occurs workers and farmers alike will not only suffer a reduction in real income, but will bring upon themselves and the nation the unparalleled disaster of unchecked inflation.

The reason why price ceilings have not already been imposed on all food products is, as you know, that paragraph 3 of the Emergency Price Control Act prohibits such ceilings until farm prices as a whole have gone up beyond parity prices —far beyond—as high as an average of 16 per cent beyond.

Although that restriction upon establishing ceilings for farm products usually is referred to as the 110 per cent of parity limitation, it is much worse than that. The statute provides other limitations which are more drastic. Ceilings cannot be imposed, under the statute, on any product at a level below the market price on October 1, 1941, or December 15, 1941, or the average price for the period July 1, 1919 to June 30,

1929, or below 110 per cent of current parity, whichever of those four levels is highest. As a result, the lowest average level for all farm commodities at which ceilings may be imposed is not 110 per cent, but 116 per cent of parity—some of the commodities going almost as high as 150 per cent of parity.

Even more important is the psychological effect of such unfair privilege. It provides fuel for fires of resentment against farmers as a favored class. After all, parity is, by its very definition, a fair relationship between the prices of the things farmers sell and the things they buy. Calculations of parity must include all costs of production including the cost of labor. As a result parity prices may shift every time wage rates shift. Insisting that the ceilings on no farm commodity shall ever be lower than 110 per cent of parity is asking for more than a fair price relationship with other prices.

In fact, the limitations on agricultural ceilings are now being cited by other groups as a reason for resisting economic controls that are needed in their own fields. The limitations will be a rallying point for such opposition as long as they are in effect.

WAGE POLICY IN THE DEFENSE PROGRAM [2]

The question of wage policy is a perennial one in capitalistic society, but it attracts popular attention primarily in periods of wide business-cycle swings. Thus in any period of sharply rising or falling business activity, accompanied by rather pronounced swings in prices and costs, the question of proper wage policy becomes a subject of active, and frequently hot, debate. It is not surprising, therefore, that the defense program with its rather intense business activity and rising cost of living should again thrust this question into the foreground. What wage policy should be followed in the present defense emergency program? Should wages be increased, and if so, by how much? Should a "ceiling" as well as a "floor" be placed

[2] By E. B. McNatt, University of Illinois. *Southern Economic Journal.* 8: 504-12. April, 1942.

on wages? Should wages be geared rather rigidly to some kind of cost-of-living index? And would this arrangement help keep down rising prices and inflation and thus protect labor's real wage from impairment? What wage policy would best facilitate the shift from defense to nondefense production when the present emergency has passed?

These and other questions seem to indicate the need for a carefully formulated national wage policy. The peculiar nature and importance of wages in our economic system, however, makes the formulation of such a national wage policy no simple or easy matter. In the first place wages represent a cost of production to industry and as such must be given careful consideration in any wage earners and as such they influence very directly consumer demand and purchasing power, which in turn, of course, influence very directly the course of the business cycle. Third, wages in a price economy measure the relative well-being of the wage earner group; their standard of living fluctuates more or less directly with the wages received. An examination and appraisal of certain current proposed wage policies in the defense period may thus be worth while.

Recently attention has been directed to Canada's wartime wage policy with the idea that it might serve as a guide to American defense wage policy. Presumably this Canadian wage policy does two things: it establishes a "ceiling" on wage rates, (i.e., the highest wage rates prevailing between 1926 and December, 1940); and it establishes a "floor" below which wages cannot fall (i.e., cost-of-living bonuses to prevent the workers' real wage from being impaired by rising living costs). This wartime wage policy avowedly has a two-fold objective: first, by setting a "ceiling" on wage rates, to stop or limit inflation; and second, by setting a "floor" under wages, to stabilize real wages at or near existing levels for the duration. Let us examine this wage policy briefly from the point of view of its objectives.

Will limiting wage advances to cost-of-living changes prevent inflation? It is said that if no ceiling is placed on wages, inflation is inevitable, inasmuch as the demands of a wartime economy will create a smaller and smaller supply of consumer goods, which, coupled with rising wage rates, will necessarily bring about rapid price advances. All of this may be granted. But will limiting wage advances to cost-of-living changes prevent such price increases? Of course, in so far as this policy holds down wage increases below those which might take place in the absence of any such limitations, it will be a factor in keeping prices from rising as fast as they otherwise would. But there are several other considerations that must be kept in mind in judging how far such limitations on wage increases as are prescribed in the Canadian plan will check inflation. In the first place a wage bonus of 5 per cent every three months would allow a maximum wage increase of 20 per cent per year. And presumably a wage bonus of 50 per cent or even 150 per cent would be payable if the cost of living advanced that fast within the year. If the increasing shortage of consumer goods is the cause of the rising cost of living, would not such wage increases as are permitted under the Canadian plan stimulate that vicious spiral of wage-price increases that this plan seeks to avoid?

Two other important considerations involved in the question of how far the cost-of-living bonuses will hold down inflation are: (1) the proportion of the Canadian wage bill paid to workers earning less than $25 per week as against the proportion paid to workers earning more than $25, and (2) the question of overtime. Inasmuch as the maximum bonus was fixed at $1.25 per week in the original Order in Council, this represented more than a 5 per cent wage increase for those earning less than $25 per week and less than 5 per cent wage increase for those earning more than $25 per week. Thus if there is a much larger proportion of the wage bill paid out to workers earning less than $25 per week, rather than to those earning more than $25, it would greatly increase the tendency toward inflation inasmuch as their money wage would be increasing faster than the cost of living. If the reverse of this were true, of course, it would represent a strong deflationary influence. The cost-of-living bonus furthermore would not check in any way a strong inflationary tendency caused by rather general overtime payments. The Canadian plan only contemplates stabilizing real basic wage rates.

Finally, it must be remembered that wages are not the only source of consumer purchasing power. While it is true that from two-thirds to three-fourths of the national income in this country and in Canada is paid out in the form of wages and salaries, income in the form of profits, interest, and rent also reaches consumer hands. Although the Canadian plan contemplates rather rigid control of these other income streams (primarily through heavy taxation), unless they are held within rather narrow limits the wage policy will be largely nullified as a device for holding down consumer purchasing power and checking inflation.

The second objective of this plan is the maintenance of real wages at or near existing levels for the duration of the war, thus preserving and protecting living standards of the wage earners. How successful this part of the plan will be depends largely upon how far the wage-increase limitations prevent or check inflation. As was pointed out above, if wartime demands continue to shrink the volume of consumer goods, there is nothing in the Canadian wage policy that can prevent rising prices, rising cost of living, and falling real wages. And regardless of this development, some deterioration of real wages and living standards seems inevitable. For example, there will always be some lag in wage-income behind cost-of-living advances, even with quarterly adjustments. If the cost of living has not advanced at least 1 per cent there will be no adjustment. And, more important, not all living standards are protected equally against impairment by this plan—only those in the lower wage class. The maximum cost-of-living bonus provided is 25 cents per week for each increase of 1 per cent in the cost of living. This is 1 per cent of $25. For wage earners earning above $100 per month therefore, their standard of living is protected against impairment only to the extent of the first $100. For wage earners receiving less than $100 per month the real wage and standard of living will presumably be maintained inasmuch as they will receive a 1 per cent bonus for each 1 per cent increase in living costs. Again, therefore, how far wage-earner living standards will be maintained or decreased will depend upon the proportion of wage earners receiving less than $25 per week in comparison with the proportion receiving more than this amount. And lastly it should be remembered that the compulsory cost-of-living bonus does not apply to all employees. Government employees, farmers, fishermen, domestic employees in private homes, casual employees, and employees of nonprofit institutions are not covered under the present plan.

The recent proposal of railroad executives to base employee wage advances in the defense period on cost-of-living changes, together with the adoption by a considerable number of firms of some kind of a cost-of-living guide to wage policy, indicates that this principle is receiving serious current attention in the formulation of American wage policy. What are the merits and limitations of a cost-of-living guide to wage policy? How far is it acceptable in the present defense program as a guide to wage policy?

An appraisal of any wage policy should stipulate clearly at the outset whether such policy is being appraised as a temporary, emergency policy or as a long-run, permanent policy. One's judgment of a policy such as a cost-of-living base for wage determination might, therefore, be altogether different when considered as a temporary, emergency plan in contrast to a long-run, permanent plan. The Canadian plan is a wartime emergency measure and should be appraised on that basis. As a wartime, temporary policy it may have some merit in helping to achieve the objectives sought. Most of the American cost-of-living plans proposed and in effect, however, have not been presented as temporary, emergency plans but instead contemplate the establishment of some kind of cost-of-living base as a rather long-run, permanent plan for making wage adjustments.

The principal merit of a cost-of-living base for making wage adjustments is that it may hold down arbitrary and unreasonable demands for wage increases or decreases. Thus it would appear to provide some yardstick with which to measure or judge the reasonableness of wage demands. But beyond this point, the usefulness of a cost-of-living index as a guide to wage policy is subject to rather sharp limitations. A brief enumeration of some of these limitations may be pertinent at this time.

In the first place the usefulness of a cost-of-living index as a guide to wage policy is generally limited largely to periods of business upswing. It is in these periods, so its advocates say, that this guide to wage policy works with its greatest effectiveness. As a matter of fact neither the Canadian plan nor the proposed American railroad plan provide for any reduction of wages below their present levels, regardless of cost-of-living changes downward. A guide to wage policy that works only one way, i.e., in periods of rising prices and business activity, may well be subject to some question as even a temporary policy, and much more so as a long-run, permanent policy. Some of the limitations of this policy as a control measure and as a real wage stabilizer in periods of business upswings were indicated above in the discussion of the Canadian plan.

Second, as a sole guide to a long-run wage policy, adjusting wages to cost-of-living changes gives no recognition to labor's changing value-productivity. According to modern wage theory, in a competitive price economy, wages should reflect, at least in some rough way, labor's value-productivity. If wages were tied rigidly to some cost-of-living base, there would be no possibility of any material labor progress,—no possibility of labor's real wage or standard of living ever advancing—regardless of possibly great increases in labor's productivity. And it is no answer to say that if labor cannot progress under this plan, neither can it retrogress. In a period of sharply falling prices and business activity industrial profits in general will tend to decline much more rapidly than the cost of living. Wage cuts in all probability could not be limited to cost-of-living decreases if business continued to operate at all. If cost-of-living decreases set the maximum limit on wage cuts during periods of severe business recession, labor's real income would fall in terms of greatly reduced employment. In a profit economy, therefore, a cost-of-living guide to wage policy might prevent labor from sharing in advancing labor productivity and real national income, but it could not prevent labor's real income from declining in a period of severe business recession. In other words, in a capitalistic society wages may lag behind labor's value-productivity for a considerable period of time, and a cost-of-living base for wage adjustments might accentuate this lag, but real wages cannot lag much behind falling labor productivity in a period of business decline.

As a corollary of the above point, it should be mentioned that a cost-of-living base gives no recognition to employer profits in determining wages. The ability of industry to pay has long been regarded as having at least some weight in making wage adjustments. There are marginal, small-profit, low-wage firms as well as prosperous, large-profit, high-wage firms in an economy. As a practical matter, differences in costs and profits between industries and between plants would not permit a rigid adherence to a cost-of-living base as a sole guide to wage policy.

Third, a more important shortcoming of the cost-of-living guide to wage policy is the fact that it has little or no value in establishing basic wage rates in the first instance,—even if all labor were the same quality or grade. Of even less value would this guide be in determining wage differentials for different grades of labor. This policy would not, therefore, eliminate the necessity for collective bargaining in the determination of basic wage rates, to say nothing of bargaining over nonwage matters such as hours, working rules, closed shop policy, etc. Thus this policy would obviously not insure industrial peace. It would not even remove wage disagreements as a cause of industrial disputes. Some lag will always be present in adjusting wages to rising cost on the upswing, and strong labor resistence to wage cuts in business downswings will be inevitable in view of the inherent urge to maintain living standards.

Fourth, a cost-of-living base for wage adjustments will not insure the maintenance of labor standards or real wages for all workers. No acceptable cost-of-living index could be broad enough to recognize the great variations in living costs between geographic localities. Some wage earners will have their incomes increased more than the cost-of-living; others will receive less. Nor could any acceptable cost-of-living index guarantee the maintenance of real wages for all workers because of the great variation in individual incomes. Any practical plan for adjusting wages to cost of living must use some wage-level as a base. Canada thus uses $25 per week as a base; the proposed American railroad plan uses $130 per month. Thus those receiving incomes higher than the base would find their real wages were diminishing, while those receiving incomes lower than the base would find their real wages were being maintained or increased.

Finally, the economic and social desirability of tying wages rigidly to cost-of-living changes may well be questioned as a long-run wage policy in view of certain functional aspects of wages in a price economy. Disregarding for the moment the functional aspect of wages as an incentive to output, and considering wages merely as a product of the labor market, how much flexibility *vs.* rigidity should wage rates have? Is it not inevitable that supply and demand factors may necessitate fluctuations in wage rates, entirely independent of cost-of-living changes, in order to redistribute the labor supply in accordance with industrial or national needs? To meet the needs of the defense program, and to take care of labor shortages and surpluses growing out of seasonal, cyclical, or secular changes in industry, some fluctuation in wage rates, regardless of cost-of-living changes, seems to be demanded. To insure its smooth functioning a competitive price economy in general needs more flexibility in its price structure rather than less.

What wage policy should be followed in the defense period? An acceptable wage policy should include at least the three following objectives: (1) as a control measure to help hold down a runaway period of inflation; (2) as a protective measure to help maintain labor's real wage and standard of living; (3) as an emergency measure to help ease the post-defense readjustment period. A national wage policy based on changing living costs would not meet these objectives. As was indicated above, so far as higher living costs are the product of a limited supply of consumer goods owing to the production of defense materials, higher wages based on these higher living costs would not solve the problem of rising prices; it would only aggravate this difficulty. Such a policy would insure the economy neither against inflation nor against impairment of labor's standard of living. It would probably be of little value in aiding the post-defense readjustment period.

The principal reliance for keeping down prices, profits, cost of living, and the necessity for wage advances in the defense period must be placed on governmental fiscal policy. The government must exert every effort to control prices by limiting consumer demand to the country's capacity to produce nondefense goods. This means that heavy taxation and widespread sales of baby bonds to consumers and wage earners must be used to dry up excess consumer purchasing power from whatever source derived. If this is successful the question of wage policy in the defense period will be more or less answered. Only such wage changes as are necessary to equalize demand and supply in the labor market will be needed. No guide to wage policy such as cost of living or employer profits would be pertinent.

In so far as government fiscal policy fails to control prices, business profits, and living costs, Professor Slichter has suggested that labor's share in these temporary profits should take the form of temporary bonuses rather than permanent wage-rate increases. Such wage increases should probably take the form of bonuses paid in national defense bonds, to be held in trust for the employee until the emergency is over. If this policy were followed it would serve the dual purpose of holding down consumer purchasing power and aiding the post-defense readjustment period. Permanent wage-rate increases would increase the difficulties of the post-defense readjustment period because they would be likely to create cost-price relationships unfavorable to employment and early business recovery. The liquidation of these bonds in the post-defense period would stimulate consumer demand at a time when it would be greatly needed.

A strong case can be made for Mr. J. M. Keynes' wage-deferment plan as a national wage policy, especially if governmental efforts in the field of taxation and voluntary savings fail to hold down prices, profits, and living costs. Roughly this plan provides for a diversion of a portion of the earnings of labor into a governmentally controlled account as a wage credit for the employed worker. In conjunction with high income taxes, the schedule of deferred wage payments would help limit consumer demand to the smaller supply of consumer goods. Moreover, the scale of taxes and deferred payments would be applied not only progressively but with the proportion taken as tax to rise sharply as income rises. This plan has the merit of meeting fairly well the three objectives suggested as necessary parts of a national wage policy. It is aimed in the first place to reducing consumer purchasing power in a period of consumer goods shortage, thus helping reduce inflationary influences. Second, it has as a definite part of its objective the idea of smoothing the transition from a war or defense economy to a peacetime economy. The wage payments withheld during the war would be released in the postwar readjustment period, thus bolstering consumer demand at a time when it is needed most. Third, this plan contemplates protecting the real incomes of the lowest groups by a progressive scale and a system of family allowances, and for all groups by keeping the cost of living from skyrocketing.

Although the Keynes plan was not adopted in England owing to the opposition of both the Labour and Conservative parties, and despite Mr. Keynes' belief that his plan is not particularly needed in the American defense program at the moment, it should be given serious consideration in the formulation of national wage policy. The alternatives to some such plan as this are grim indeed—either inflation with all its injustices and hardships or rigid governmental price controls with possibly strict rationing of all consumer goods.

The present price-control bill being considered in Congress provides for rather rigid control of all prices except wages and the prices of farm commodities. The principal argument for including wages in any omnibus price-control measure has stressed the importance of wages as a cost of production,—that if wages are uncontrolled prices will have to advance in order to cover the higher costs of production. This will lead to demands for higher wages to cover increased living costs, which will again send prices skyrocketing. In support of this argument the Brookings Institution has pointed out that average weekly earnings in 90 manufacturing industries increased 26 per cent between July, 1940, and July, 1941. The increase in rates of pay and employment together raised the total wage payments in these industries 55 per cent in the first year of the defense program. During the same period the cost of living rose about 7 per cent and manufacturing profits increased about 16 per cent.

In rebuttal to this argument labor has stressed the fact that higher wages do not necessarily mean higher labor costs, that increasing labor productivity may offset any tendency toward higher unit labor costs and that the proportion of labor costs to total costs is rather low in many industries.

There are certainly elements of truth in both of these propositions. But it would appear that they both miss the much more vital issue in the problem of wage and price control, namely, the consideration of wages and profits as distributive shares influencing consumer demand rather than consideration of wages primarily as a cost of production. The strongest argument for some wage- and price-control measure in the defense period centers around the necessity for limiting consumer demand. It is therefore extremely doubtful how far government price fixing would be successful as an effective device for controling prices, wages, profits, and cost of living. Controls must be exercised primarily through limitations of demand.

Entirely aside from the question of desirability of some wage-control measure, the administrative problems involved in an attempt to enforce rigid wage limits would be tremendous. The usually suggested controls would "freeze" existing wage situations for the duration of the emergency. But there is no suggestion that workers be prevented from moving from places and industries where wages are lower to those where they are higher. And if employers wished to make some wage advances beyond those specified in a wage-control law—say to attract new workers or hold existing workers—they could do so by promotions, reclassifications, bonuses, overtime, etc.—none of which would be prohibited under most proposed "wage-freezing" plans.

In conclusion the following summary may be offered. One, as long as the national income and profits are increasing, some wage increases are desirable. Limitation upon wages should not be instituted until the demands of the defense program make it impossible to produce both "guns and butter," and until profits of industry are restricted in the same proportion as the contemplated wage restriction. Two, a cost-of-living guide to wage policy, such as the Canadian plan or suggested American plans, is wholly inadequate either as a temporary, wartime policy or as a permanent, peacetime plan. Even as a supplement to high taxes and voluntary savings, such a policy will not secure the ends sought. Three, the first reliance for controlling wages, prices, profits, and cost of living should be placed upon government fiscal policy. Taxation and voluntary savings should be the first line of attack upon inflation and rising costs of living. Four, if governmental fiscal policy fails to limit consumer demand to the country's capacity to produce nondefense goods, a national wage policy based on some kind of wage-deferment plan should receive serious consideration. And finally, any wage policy that eventually emerges from the defense period should preferably be the result of agreement among representatives of labor, industry, and the government, rather than imposed upon labor and industry by the government. Governmental compulsion in the establishment of a national wage policy should be undertaken only as a last resort.

WAGE ADJUSTMENTS IN THIS WAR [3]

The exigencies of war continually and profoundly alter labor policies and practices, not least those pertaining to wages. Many of the policies required by national interests during a great war are almost the exact opposities of policies appropriate

[3] By Z. Clark Dickinson, Professor of Economics, University of Michigan. *Annals of the American Academy*. 224:62-8. November, 1942.

to a chronic depression like that of the 1930's. One oft-recurring suggestion as to how wages should be handled in wartime, to be sure, would make this present article superfluous: I mean the demand that all wages, prices, and rents be simply frozen for the war's duration. If this plan were literally adopted, the subject of wage adjustments during the war would become quite academic, like the essay on "Snakes in Ireland" which began categorically: "There are no snakes in Ireland." But such simple and universal freezing of wages is most unlikely to be continued, if undertaken; and we may confidently assume that many better and worse wage adjustments will continue to be made.

Several of the moot points in this field were brought into focus by the War Labor Board's policy enunciated in the recent Little Steel cases, in which a 5½-cent rise in wage rates was granted, on the ground that this boost, together with previous wage increases, would make the relative advance in wage rates since January 1941 at least equal to the relative rise in living costs in steel centers. Was this a proper application of the wage clauses and implications of the President's anti-inflation program? What other government agencies, if any, should participate in shaping and implementing our national wage policy? Are "parity wages" indefinitely to chase "parity prices" uphill? During this war, what is happening to collective bargaining? Should government wage control be extended from *minimum-wage* determinations, only to wage fixations *incident to labor disputes*, or should public authorities also establish *maximum* wage rates or ceilings—even where no labor-capital controversy has arisen? Must wages be determined fundamentally by irrational political pressures and maneuvers of various factions for power? Such are a few of the current controversies relevant to wages.

Let us approach a review of the facts and outlook in our own country from the angle of nations which were earlier swept fully into the present war. After the extreme inflations following 1918, Europeans were willing to accept extreme measures to prevent recurrence of such troubles. Nazi measures of price and wage control, for example, were totalitarian and effective from the onset of the party's power. Soon after the present war began in 1939, the current of anti-inflation opinion in English-speaking countries was accelerated by publication and discussions of the Keynes Plan.

The influence of this agitation, though indirect, has been very considerable. In Britain and elsewhere, compulsory war loans became practical politics; and labor as well as other public opinion is much better informed than it was a generation ago as to the inflationary possibilities of the attempt fully to maintain real wage rates. The British wartime compulsory arbitration law has had little occasion to be used, and wage rates and prices have advanced much more slowly than in World War I.

Canadian wage and price policies have also reflected various parts of Keynes's analysis, in ways that might be expected in view of the weaker position of organized labor in the Dominion's political life. Far-reaching steps have been taken toward authoritative ceilings over *all* wages, not merely over those involved in labor disputes. Widespread and fairly effective controls have been placed upon prices and rents. The wage policy provides two elements of elasticity: (1) low-paid labor may have its wages advanced, from time to time, more or less commensurately with any advance in the special cost-of-living index, and higher-paid workers simultaneously obtain only the same *absolute* cost-of-living bonus; (2) otherwise wage rates were frozen at prewar levels except where it could be established that the prewar rate was unduly depressed in relation to similar work in other establishments.

Let us now summarize and assess the chief practices and theories of recent wage adjustments in the United States.

A review of pertinent American events may begin with the respective behaviors of indexes of wage rates and prices. During 1914-16, just before our country entered World War I, these indexes in the United States rose only some 7 or 8 per cent. Over the years 1939-41, by contrast, our wage rates increased distinctly more than did the index of living costs. In mid-1939, for example, average hourly earnings in all manufacturing were about 64 cents per hour, near the peak they had reached in the heyday of C.I.O. organization in 1935-37; and by January 1941 the corresponding average had advanced nearly to 69 cents, while the index of living costs had scarcely changed. By April 1942 average hourly earnings in all manufacturing had climbed further almost to 82 cents, thereby gaining nearly 20 per cent over January 1941, while the index of living costs advanced some 15 per cent. Some of this rise, of course, is attributable to the general 50-per-cent-penalty overtime rate, and overtime worked was very unequally distributed; but in much greater measure it was due to rises in straight-time rates. Prices and nonwage incomes also advanced, yet the percentage which all (nonrelief) wage and salary earnings formed of the total national income was trending upward after 1939.

It seems, then, that American labor participated more promptly in the general rise of money incomes at the outset of the present war than it did in World War I. The increase in hourly earnings cited above did not, in 1939-40, raise unit labor costs in equal measure, since most plants were being worked at greater percentages of their capacities. As this slack was taken up, however, further rises in hourly earnings signified more direct upward pressure on prices.

By mid-1941 the growth of national-defense consciousness had accelerated the progress of pledges by labor to avert strikes, and the public became increasingly aware that such good resolutions had the best chance of success if public authorities developed wise leadership toward preventing and settling labor disputes. The National Defense Mediation Board made a good start in this direction. One significant trend in this period is indicated by the following statement: "Voluntary wage stabilization agreements are now in effective operation in the shipbuilding and construction industries, covering more than 2,500,000 workers." Various unions outside the A.F.L. also participated, as well as high government officials.

Two points involved in this phase of wage stabilization were: (1) such leveling-up and rationalization of the wage structure through the industry or local sections as could be at once achieved; and (2) agreement that further wage rises would not be sought within six months, nor then, unless advancing living costs justified new demands. These arrangements are important milestones in labor-relations statesmanship; but it soon became evident that more comprehensive and teeth-bearing controls of prices, wages, and other economic factors had become necessary.

Soon after Pearl Harbor the outstanding labor organizations gave sweeping no-strike pledges, and early in January 1942 the National War Labor Board was established to settle labor disputes which resisted other treatment and which threatened the war effort. On January 30, 1942, the Price Control Act was signed, containing a clause little noticed at the time, directing W.L.B. and other government agencies concerned with wages "within the limits of their authority and jurisdiction, to work toward a stabilization of prices, fair and equitable wages and cost of production." On April 27 a more explicit statement of government policy on wages was made by President Roosevelt in the course of his seven-point anti-inflation program. He advocated "stabilization" of wage rates, cautioning W.L.B., however, to "continue to give due consideration to inequalities and the elimination of substandards of living."

This pronouncement could reasonably be interpreted as endorsing the spirit, at least, of W.L.B.'s previous action (April 15) on wages of International Harvester Company workers. In this decision the Board said:

> The real wage levels which have been previously arrived at through the channels of collective bargaining and which do not impede maximum production of war materials shall be reasonably protected. This does not mean that labor can expect to receive throughout the war upward changes in its wage structure which will enable it to keep pace with upward changes in the cost of living.

On July 16 the same Board decided the Little Steel cases. Instead of the increase of 12.5 cents an hour asked by the steel workers, the Board awarded an advance of 5.5 cents, on substantially the following grounds: (1) In addition to wage advances already won, the steel workers required a rise of 3.2 cents per hour to bring their real hourly rates up to the level of January 1941, on the basis of the national average rise of 15 per cent in living costs; and (2) Because living costs had increased more than this in steel centers, also because this case had been opened several weeks before the President's statement of policy on April 27, 2.3 cents more were awarded—total 5.5 cents.

As usual, this decision on wage rates was accompanied by settlements of various other matters in dispute. The union was given much of what it desired in the way of alteration of certain wage payment plans, "union security," and check-off of dues.

The employees, the fact-finding panel, and the labor members of the Board devoted much attention to the argument that total weekly earnings of steel workers had fallen behind those in other industries in which more overtime was worked, and they pointed out that the companies concerned were now so prosperous that they would have little incentive to try to pass along higher wages in higher prices—it would be much simpler to pay less excess profits taxes to the government. The majority of the Board, however, had already found hourly wage rates usually the most suitable common denominator among companies and industries, and it said in this case:

> What the Board must not do, and what it avoids doing in this case, is to start another lap in the race between prices and wages. Another cycle of general wage increases started at this time would seriously threaten the chance to stabilize the cost of living.

This view presupposed that most wage rates already had advanced at least as much, or nearly as much, as 15 per cent since January 1941. It is not yet clear how far this presupposition is in accord with fact.

A few days later (July 20) the American Federation of Labor issued a Declaration on Wages and Inflation, which constitutes the latest milestone to be noticed in the present article. It is a well-considered program, including suggestions for cost controls on war contracts, increasing social security taxes, and establishment of a representative national wage-policy commission. One significant proposal was also put forward by labor in the Little Steel cases—that some wage increases might be paid in war bonds, cashable after the war. By this means labor adapts part of the Keynes Plan, arguing that "deferred pay" cannot have inflationary effect during the war.

So much for a brief recital of relevant American events. Let us now explore further their significance. It will be useful first to summarize the broad principles which are widely accepted, and then to analyze the puzzles and ambiguities involved in their practical application, in relation to the machinery which is in sight for wage adjustments.

No important group has seriously objected to the general principles outlined by the President on April 27. Nearly everyone approves in principle of endeavors to fight inflation and profiteering by either property or labor. The President's hints as to applications of these principles, too, have met with widespread agreement. No large section of our nonlabor public appears to want wages frozen as hard as in the Canadian policy; on the other hand, our organized labor appears to join in demands for wage "stabilization." Exceptionally low-paid or "substandard" labor's wages are still to be leveled upward, and other "inequities" are to be corrected, in part by wage increases. In order to rush resources into the more urgently needed war industries, the profit motive must be given some scope with respect to labor as well as capital—high wages, bonuses, salaries, profits, must be added to the other incentives which divert productive powers into bomber plants, shipyards, ship crews, at optimum speed. Overwhelming majorities of workers and managers adjourn their normal rights to suspend production, and support the compulsions applied by public authorities against the few recalcitrants. Strong efforts are made to root out wasteful practices by managements and antisocially restrictive rules of labor. New doors are opened to minority groups. These are familiar yet vital elements of the environment of wartime wage policy.

We need not dig far beneath the surface, of course, to discover many ambiguities and disputes as to the proper applications of these accepted principles. Prominent among unsettled matters are the degrees in which real wage rates can and should be maintained, and the procedures which are most likely to accomplish the needful maintenance. An outstanding thread which runs through both these problems is the question of real-wage ceilings and floors.

The question of real-wage maintenance involves numerous subsidiary issues, including controls of other incomes. Some incisive comments along this line were made by the employer members of W.L.B. in the Little Steel decision:

> Any wage stabilization program, to be effective, must go hand-in-hand with a price fixing program, a price fixing of all commodities, including farm products. Industry has already accepted price ceilings imposed upon its products; labor must likewise accept a wage ceiling. . . . Industry cannot ask labor to accept stabilization of wages unless it also is prepared to accept a general stabilization of all salaries and bonuses. As to salaries, the President has indicated, and with this we concur, that the practical way to accomplish this is through the income tax machinery. . . .

Not all the necessary controls can practicably be worked out at once; some groups must inevitably make sacrifices ahead of others. But it is clear enough that some sorts of wage ceilings are required to make effective price control feasible; also that labor's full cooperation is dependent upon visible results in curbing profiteering in non-wage incomes. Meanwhile it must be expected that the Office of Price Administration will attempt rather sweepingly to restrain wage advances, for each one is a threat to price stabilization; that W.L.B. will take a more optimistic view as to how much its latest correction of "inequities" by leveling wages upward will crowd prices skyward; and that labor should press its solution of wage increases paid in war bonds and should overlook the tendency of each wage advance to provoke others. It is our collective national responsibility to improvise continuously a total wage policy compatible with our policy of controls, taxes, and war loans in respect to all incomes.

An outstanding criterion for this over-all policy on wartime wages is total wage payments in relation to the whole national income. Considering the much higher level of employment during wartime, it appears reasonable that labor's share (before taxes) should run higher than in peacetime; and that taxation and compulsory war loans should become more steeply progressive to pay for the war.

The dangers of inflation are so great, however, that wage rises to relieve substandard workers and to remove inequities should be awarded conservatively, and public officials should avoid creating expectations that *if*, unfortunately, the cost of living rises further, all wage earners who make sufficient fuss will have their wage rates raised *in proportion to such advance in living costs.* Higher social-security contributions, and wage increments paid in war bonds, are *comparatively* noninflationary methods of advancing real wages. They give their beneficiaries no immediate increase of purchasing power. On the other hand, they mark up the employer's costs, and thereby tend to boost prices.

Some further important considerations of national wage policy may be conveniently brought out through a review of our wage adjustment machinery. A key to both matters is that we are better equipped for settling wage disputes than for determining proper wage floors and ceilings in situations where disputes do not arise. Thus, opposite extremes are neglected. Low-paid workers who are supposed to be protected by minimum-wage laws find such protection slipping as the purchasing power of 30 to 40 cents an hour declines. On the other hand, employers paying excess-profits taxes may raise wages almost at will, at little expense to the incomes left to them after taxes.

We appear much more alive to the latter of these problems. The War Manpower Commission (W.M.C.), the United States Employment Service (U.S.E.S.), and the War Labor Board have made various moves toward restraining "labor piracy" and inflationary wage advances outside of labor disputes, but the brunt seems to have been borne thus far by O.P.A. Any individual who aspires to high elective office in the future hesitates to restrain labor from getting all it can by voluntary collective bargaining.

What reorganization and reorientation is needed among our wage fixers? Various proposals are put forward from time to time for creation of a new czar of wages, and the A.F.L.'s, cited above, is but one of several projects for a wage or labor policy board. It is difficult to see that the national interest could be served by undermining an agency so vital and effective as W.L.B. In the long run it may, indeed, be desirable for our nation to have a full-time supreme tribunal for labor disputes. A separate representative policy or advisory board might supplement such an agency very well. But don't swap horses while fording such a deep stream as this war! The individual representatives of labor and of employers on W.L.B. are, or should be, drawn from nominees of suitable organizations. Thus the demand for a policies board is met in part, and the labor and employer organizations do, or should, feel directly responsible for acts of their members on the board. Of course, the numerous groups, public and private, which are concerned with wages should consult frequently and attempt continuously to improve the aggregate of policies and practices involved.

Restraint of voluntary wage increases beyond reasonable ceilings will continue to be sought by several means, which should have organic connections with the opposite problem of wage floors. O.P.A.'s price controls, for example, may be administered so as both to discourage unduly high labor costs and to broadcast information on current minimum wage standards. As government agencies such as W.M.C. and U.S.E.S. acquire increasing conscriptive powers, they should also assume the obligation to see that labor thus requisitioned for national service is reasonably paid. In fact, W.M.C. already has exerted pressure toward leveling up wage rates in some occupations and industries. A third avenue for extending wage controls is to bring various voluntary labor agreements within the authority of W.L.B. If this last method were used exclusively to maintain wage ceilings it would be much more offensive to labor, and to liberal opinion generally, than if it followed the trend started long ago by New Zealand's "extension of collective agreements," which principle is roughly illustrated by the labor provisions of our Guffey coal acts.

The main idea is public enforcement of collective agreements (particularly upon unorganized sections of industries), *so far as the public authorities find the terms of such agreements in the public interest.* Labor seems likely to accept, without too much opposition, reasonable wage ceilings under such inquiries if the public authorities are simultaneously raising some wage floors outside of wage disputes and beyond the older apparatus of legal minimum wages.

WLB VIEWS ON WAGE STABILIZATION [4]

Even before the President spoke on April 27, the [National War Labor] Board had already outlined at least some of the basic problems it would have to face. By the time of the International Harvester decision, about the middle of April, it had already made up its mind on several things.

The first of these was that substandard wages were a threat to effective production, not only because they affect morale adversely but because they have a deleterious effect on health and so tend to lower productive efficiency. Substandard wages, therefore, will be raised by the War Labor Board in the interests of the war effort.

The Board has not yet defined, or attempted to define, what it considers a substandard wage; but once it has determined that a given wage is substandard, there is no question that, regardless of ability to pay, the wage will be raised.

Moreover, the Board had concluded, even before the President spoke, that certain types of inequalities or inequities—maladjustments in the wage structure—would have to be corrected. This also is in the interest of the war effort as such inequities lower morale or result in a maldistribution or a mischanneling of the labor supply, or hinder the efforts of the unions to keep the men on the job.

Before the President spoke, the Board had also come to the clear realization that real wages could not, in most cases, be maintained for the duration, that the cost of living at that time was rising faster than wages could hope to rise. And although the Board said in the International Harvester case that it did

[4] By Ralph T. Seward, Associate Public Member, National War Labor Board. From pamphlet "Wage Stabilization and Adjustment." p. 3-10. Personnel Series No. 61. American Management Association. New York. 1942.

not want to put labor in a straitjacket—that to fix wages while the cost of living continued to rise would have a seriously adverse effect on the war effort—still the Board recognized clearly in that decision that wages could not, by and large, hope to keep up with an unrestricted rise in the cost of living.

It was at that stage in the evolution of the Board's ideas that the President delivered his message of April 27, in which he directed the Board to continue to eliminate substandard wages and certain inequalities. But he changed the situation to some extent when he said, "I will now stabilize the cost of living, and on the basis of that stabilization I believe that wages can and should be maintained at existing scales." And he asked the Board to maintain them there.

That presented the Board with quite a problem. What did the President mean by "existing scales"? Briefly, the Board found from its examinations of statistics that there had been from, roughly, the beginning of 1937 until 1941 a relative stability. There were some fluctuations, it is true, but a comparatively stable relationship between wages and prices existed during that period; the rise in both wages and prices which resulted from the transfer of our economy to a war production basis really began shortly after January 1, 1941. Between that time and the date of the President's message, there had been approximately a 15.1 per cent rise in the cost of living. However, the rise in wages had been by no means so uniform: Some wages had gone far ahead of the cost of living, increasing by 25 or 30 per cent; others had fallen behind or had not advanced at all.

The Board said: "We will stabilize on the basis of the real wages from straight-time hourly earnings as of January 1, 1941, the most recent date of real stability. Wages which have already advanced as much or more than 15 per cent will not be further increased. Wages which have not already advanced that much will be raised, under ordinary circumstances, to at least that point."

As to the effectiveness of that formula, there has been a great deal of argument. And there will be more if its use is continued under the new setup. However, certain things may be said for it.

In the first place, the Board reached its decision only after the most careful examination of the figures and the estimates of the best experts with which the government could supply us, experts from the Bureau of Labor Statistics. At the outside, even if one figures on not merely a 15 per cent increase for those whose wages have not kept pace with the cost of living, but an 18 per cent increase, to do away with substandards and inequalities—even on that basis the increase in the wage bill would be something less than a billion dollars, which is approximately 3 per cent of the total wage bill. The Board does not feel, and I do not believe anyone else can seriously argue, that such a limited increase would have an inflationary effect. If we can stabilize on that basis, we shall have done a good job.

In the second place, there is no question but that wages and salaries have gone up extraordinarily during the last two or three years; the rise, on the base of 1939, is 68.5 per cent. But there are two things to remember about that increase: First, that figure includes salaries, with which of course the Board has not so far been dealing. Second, during that time employment has increased 25 per cent and hours worked, 13 per cent, while overtime has increased to such an extent that, although average hourly earnings have increased only 31 per cent, average weekly earnings have gone up 55 per cent.

To the extent that there is expanding employment and an increase in the hours worked, of course, any change in the wage rates is the more serious from an inflationary standpoint. On the other hand, so far as expanding employment is concerned, we are nearing the bottom of the bucket; in some respects employment may shortly begin contracting. Much the same is true of overtime; we are reaching the point where more overtime—much more overtime, that is—cannot be added to the work week. So from now on I do not believe that increases in wage rates will have the same effect on the total wage bill as they have had in the past.

Now as to the Board's formula, several points ought to be made clear. In the first place, it is not a rigid rule. It is not something one can work out by putting figures in at one end of a machine and getting the answer out at the other end. It is not something, quite frankly (and probably unfortunately, so far as industry is concerned), which will permit an executive to sit back in his office with a paper and pencil, or possibly an adding machine, and figure out from the state of his payroll just exactly what the Board will do to his employees' wages. It is not so simple as that. It is a guiding principle; it is one of the signs that point to London; but it is not a definite answer. It is only the cost-of-living formula. It is only one of the three legs of the foot-stool on which the Board rests in every wage decision.

The Board has not only to ask itself, "Is there any ground for a wage adjustment based on a rise in the cost of living?" It has also to ask itself: "Are these wages substandard?" and "Are there inequalities or maladjustments in the wage structure which require adjustment?" And it cannot merely take those three considerations in sequence and cross-check them off. It has to consider the effect of one on the other.

For example: The Board had a case recently in which it was quite clear that on the cost-of-living basis (this was the Lever Brothers case in New Jersey) a wage increase was clearly justified—the employes had had only about a 10 per cent increase since January 1, 1941. On the other hand, it was equally clear to the Board that to grant an increase would widen the gap which already existed between Lever Brothers wages and other wages in the industry and in the area. The company was already paying top rates, and for the Board to have applied the cost-of-living formula would have been contrary to one of the other principles that the Board follows. Therefore, even though, on the basis of the cost-of-living formula alone, something like a 3 to 4 per cent wage increase was indicated, the Board refused to grant any wage increase at all rather than disturb the area and industry wages and create an inequality and a maladjustment where there had been none before.

Similarly, the elevator operators in New York had had no wage increase at all before the war broke out (there was a master agreement covering almost all large apartment, loft, and office buildings in New York). Employees were clearly entitled to 15 per cent. The Board found, however, that there had been stabilized relationships between the wages in different classes of apartments, lofts, and office buildings and between the three classes of buildings, all competing largely in the same labor market and all offering similar work. Through a series of arbitrations and decisions, stable relationships had been established in the industry. The Board felt that it was far more important to protect these stable relationships than to adhere to the strict cost-of-living formula. The Board did protect them, therefore, even though doing so meant that employees in certain classes of buildings received a somewhat smaller increase and those in other classes of buildings a somewhat larger one. Some got 11 per cent, and some got 17 per cent. But the stable relationship that was important to the industry was maintained.

We have to consider all three criteria. And it is important to remember also that the dates, January 1 and May 1, are not to be taken too literally. We received a telegram about two weeks after the formula was issued from an employer who said, "I granted a wage increase, and the contract was signed about 11:30 p.m. on December 31, 1940. Is that to be counted, or isn't it?"

Now, obviously, we are not talking in technical terms of that sort, and no one could answer that question without knowing a great deal about the situation. If the result of that wage increase had been merely to establish what should have been the existing scale in that company prior to 1941—if, in other words, the company had been at the tail end of a wage increase and the rest of the industry had gone up during 1940—the Board might have been inclined to assume that the wage increase only established an existing scale as of January 1, and to reckon the 15 per cent from that point.

If, on the other hand, this company had taken the lead in a wage increase—that is, if it were in advance of its industry—the Board might well have felt that, even though the increase had been granted, technically, somewhat before January 1, 1941, it really should be counted as a new increase, and included as part of the 15 per cent.

If, on the other hand, this company had taken the lead in a wage increase—that is, if it were in advance of its industry—the Board might well have felt that, even though the increase had been granted, technically, somewhat before January 1, 1941, it really should be counted as a new increase, and included as part of the 15 per cent.

It must be remembered also that the wage formula does not apply to individuals. The Board is talking about groups. Frankly, however, I cannot say exactly what groups the Board will average in applying its formula. It has done a great many different things in trying to find the best solution to each individual case. It may be approaching a more uniform answer, but that answer is not yet clear. It has averaged the employees in a large section of an industry, as in the Little Steel case. It has averaged the employees in a large company with many plants, as in the Aluminum Company case. It has averaged the employees in a plant—one plant of many in a company; and it has averaged the employees in an industry as a whole.

I cannot say, however, that the Board has yet reached that answer which will most effectively bridge the gap between the necessities of the anti-inflation program and the necessities of equity in a particular labor dispute.

It must be remembered that the formula applies only to straight-time average hourly earnings. It does not apply to overtime rates, premium pay and all the rest. Ordinarily, night differentials, etc., will not be included as wage increases. The formula is not, however, phrased in terms of wage rates because changes in some incentive systems, bonuses, piecework rates, etc., must be included. In centain cases we have to talk realistically in terms of average straight-time earnings, rather than in terms of rates.

Remember also that the Board is talking in terms of the national cost of living. Certain panels have misunderstood that and have recommended to the Board that since, in certain areas, there is an 18 per cent increase in the cost of living, wages should be adjusted on that basis. The Board said clearly in the recent General Motors case that its formula applies to the national average increase between those two terminal dates of January 1, 1941, and May, 1942.

One other thing: I think that industry will find as it approaches the War Labor Board, say six months from now, that it will no longer be interested in the Little Steel formula but will be extremely interested in what the Board means by "inequalities." Already a large section—some people have estimated it at three-quarters—of the large war industries has had a 15 per cent increase, or more. Other industries are getting it. That means that if the cost of living itself is held stable, so that the Board will not have to revise its position with regard to it, the cost-of-living formula will have been exhausted; and in most cases the only wage adjustment by the Board will be because of substandards, or to correct maladjustments and inequalities.

It is clear, moreover, that the Board is not thinking in terms of simple averages. "The average wage in a given industry is 72 cents for common labor; therefore, we are going to take everybody whose wages are under that and bring them up," is not the pattern we shall use. There are some differentials, many differentials in fact, which have a sound economic basis. There are some companies which pay higher wages and thereby, through the superior skill of their employees, achieve lower labor costs. There are many factors of that sort which should not be tampered with arbitrarily.

The Board does, however, consider three sorts of inequality. It will look at your wage scale if you come before it with several points in mind.

It will decide whether there are serious inequalities—maladjustments in the internal wage structure of your company, different wages for the same job. Second, it will consider the effect of your wage scale on the area wage scale; and that will, of course, bring in manpower problems and wages in the area, regardless of the industry. And third, of course, competitive wage rates in the industry will be considered.

Somehow, by balancing those three things, the Board will find the answer to your particular wage problem.

HOW MUCH TRADE-UNIONISM AS USUAL? [5]

The problem of the relation of wage policy to price control began to become acute late in 1941. During that year the total payrolls of the nation had risen about 25 per cent above the previous year, but the effect of larger incomes upon prices was partly restrained by substantial increases in the output of civilian goods. As war production expands, however, the output of civilian goods must decline. By the end of 1942, it will be at least one-fourth below the peak of 1941, and in 1943 it will go still lower. And yet the total payrolls of the country in 1942, without any increases in wage rates, will rise by another 15 per cent because of promotions, more employment, and more overtime. Profits, incidentally, in 1942 will be substantially below 1941 and probably below 1940. With payrolls rapidly rising and the supply of civilian goods dropping, prices will be in danger of skyrocketing. Wage increases simply cannot be permitted to aggravate this danger.

Neither the government nor the unions were prompt in recognizing the need for a national wage policy. The Conference on Wartime Labor Relations did not touch the question. The so-called price-control bill, passed in January, 1942, provided for little real control of farm prices and no control of wages. The War Labor Board, established early in January, carefully refrained from adopting a wage policy. The unions were demanding substantial wage increases, with 10 cents an hour or a dollar a day a typical demand. They denied that wage increases would increase the danger of inflation. They called it a reflection on the intelligence of the American worker to assume that a larger income would cause him to pay uneconomic prices for goods. The unions added that their members were entitled to higher wages in order to help them buy War Savings Bonds and thus provide a cushion against postwar depression.

There is more merit in the union arguments than most economists are prepared to admit. Certainly the greatest protection against inflation in this country up to now has been

[5] From article by Sumner H. Slichter, Mediator, Economist and Teacher. *Atlantic Monthly*. 171:75-7. January, 1943.

the unwillingness of consumers to reach for scarce goods at higher prices. And it is true that a wide distribution of the public debt would help sustain demand after the war. Nevertheless, despite the prudence which consumers have thus far shown, it would be foolhardy to widen unnecessarily the rapidly growing gap between incomes and the supply of goods.

Nor is the bond-purchase argument convincing. With the supply of goods diminishing and payrolls rising, workers, even after the payment of higher taxes, will have devoted from 20 to 25 billion dollars of surplus income by the middle of 1944 either to the reduction of their debts, or to the purchase of War Savings Bonds, or to the accumulation of cash. This is not only an adequate cushion for the postwar transition, but it is a large enough one to create the danger of an uncontrolled postwar boom.

By the end of April, the President saw that something would have to be done to control wages and prices and to impose more or less equal sacrifices on all principal groups—farmers, workers, and business owners. He asked Congress to correct the formula in the price-control bill which permitted prices of farm products to rise 10 per cent above parity or even higher. He also asked for tax increases which would reduce "discrepancies between low personal incomes and very high personal incomes." He promised to "stabilize" wages, but, curiously enough, he did not ask Congress to give him authority over wages.

In the Little Steel decision in July, the War Labor Board adopted as the standard of wage stabilization the purchasing power of wage rates on January 1, 1941—close to an all-time high for labor. Since the cost of living had increased about 15 per cent since January 1, 1941, the Board held that any group of workers which averaged less than a 15 per cent rise in hourly rates during this period would be entitled to sufficient increase to preserve the "established peacetime standards." All labor members on the Board voted against the stabilization formula. They charged that the Board had "substituted rhetoric for analysis" in going all-out "for the inflation thesis, a thesis compounded of conjectures and prophecies, fears, and hysterias. . . ."

Not until the President in his Labor Day speech threatened to act even without well-established legal authority did Congress finally tighten the loose limitations on agricultural prices. At the same time Congress gave the President an authority and a duty which he had not asked for. It "authorized and directed" him, "as far as practicable," to stabilize wages at the levels of September 15, 1942. The President promptly ordered the War Labor Board to approve no advance in wages above the rates prevailing on that date unless the increase was necessary to correct "maladjustments" or "inequalities" or to aid in the "effective prosecution of the war."

Furthermore the President appointed a Director of Economic Stabilization and an Economic Stabilization Board to advise the director. A happy stroke of wartime administration led the President to place on the Board the heads of the Farm Bureau Federation, the A.F. of L., the C.I.O., and the United States Chamber of Commerce. Only the National Association of Manufacturers and Mr. John L. Lewis, who may be regarded as the head of a third labor movement in the country, were left out. These appointments are highly significant because they place the responsibility for recommending wage and price policies largely on the leaders of the most powerful organized groups in the country. These men must see that the special interests of their respective groups are subordinated to a national policy of stabilization.

By the middle of November the National War Labor Board had five thousand cases awaiting approval—most of them increases granted voluntarily by employers. In addition, the United States Conciliation Service had thousands of disputes, mostly wage cases, which it had not certified to the War Labor Board. Many unions are assuming that the possibility of gaining wage increases to correct "maladjustments" or "inequalities" or to "aid in the effective prosecution of the war" will permit the continuance of considerable collective bargaining.

As a matter of administrative necessity the War Labor Board will have to give a narrow construction to "maladjustments," "inequalities," and "effective prosecution of the war." Otherwise it will be swamped with wage cases—for now the Board must pass on *all* wage increases, not simply the cases which reach it as disputes. Furthermore, as scarcities of goods become more acute and more pervasive, the only kind of wage changes which will make sense are those which will facilitate the great redistribution of labor required by the war. Certainly no responsible public agency will go far in giving men more dollars with which to buy goods which do not exist or which can be had in only rationed quantities.

UNCONTROLLED INFLATIONARY ITEMS [6]

The administration has never been willing to take adequate steps to control all inflationary factors. From the beginning, farm prices and wages have been exempt. It is well known that these two groups—farm and labor—are powerful politically and carry much weight in Congress. Moreover, it was held by many that farm prices ought to be allowed to rise automatically, for they had not advanced so fast or so far, on a percentage basis, as had wages under dynamic labor leadership. The administration took the attitude that wages would not advance if prices were not allowed to rise—thus removing the main cause for agitation for higher wages by labor.

Of these two potential inflationary factors, farm prices rank as number one, because of the extent to which the products of agriculture enter into the cost-of-living items. . . .

The second of the two most powerful inflationary factors was uncontrolled wages. The pressure exerted on price ceilings by wages is not so visible as that of farm prices but it is practically as strong. The effect of rising wages on the cost of living shows up in larger payrolls, which permit greater spending, and in an increase in production costs. Wages and farm prices did not increase simultaneously. Although many wage advances came in 1940 and 1941, they became a powerful inflationary force only in the last half of 1942, the main reason being that the wage advances were absorbed by the manufacturer out of the profits. In the early period of the wage increases prior

[6] From article "First Year of Price Control," by J. V. Bell, Department of Economics, University of Illinois. *Opinion and Comment.* 5:3-6. February 16, 1943.

to May, 1942, there was also an increase in the productivity of labor, which tended to offset the wage advances. Since that time, however, the rise in payrolls has not been offset by increased productivity; consequently, unit labor costs have risen sharply and steadily.

While it is true that some wages in some industries have not advanced recently, because of agreements with the administration or for other reasons, yet in wages, as in prices, there are certain "hidden advances." These take the form of "adjustments," such as extra vacations with pay, bonuses, shift premiums, overtime premiums, and so on. Since January 1, 1941, average hourly factory earnings have risen 28 per cent and the cost of living approximately 19 per cent. Average hourly earnings in the non-durable goods industries have increased 21 per cent in the same period. The relationship which exists between living costs and wage rates will not allow any perceptible increase in living costs without touching off an avalanche of demands for higher wages due to higher prices. This is an extremely vulnerable relationship.

Not all the blame for the inflationary splurge in wage rates is due to inadequate wage-control laws. The employers must bear part of the responsibility. Profits were greater than ever before and an increase in wages was no great burden to the employer. Labor shortages in practically all areas led to reprehensible competitive bidding for labor at unheard-of wages. Frequently any increase in labor costs could be passed on, since many producers were working on a cost-plus basis. The advances granted by some industries because they "felt they could do it" became contagious, thus forcing advances in others in order that workers might be kept. Since the estimate of increase in productivity of labor for the third quarter of 1942 is only 2 per cent over that for the entire year 1941, the hourly wage advances are even more severe. The government should apply to wage determination a general policy similar to that decided upon for determining and administering commodity prices. The principle of collective bargaining is at cross-purposes with the principles of price control. Huge war profits should not be a bone of contention between capital and labor. In the interest of price control, the excessive profits, if any, should be taken by the government.

It is true that steps were taken in the legislation of October, 1942, to curb inflation; however, they were neither positive nor dependable. The law would make it possible to exert some control over every sort of financial transaction—the prices of goods and services, wages, salaries, farm income, profits, subsidies, etc. Control over the two most inflationary items, namely, farm prices and wages, is limited and obscure. The law will not permit ceilings on farm prices below parity or current market prices, and in computing parity the cost increase since January, 1941, must be considered. Naturally, parity prices will be higher because of increases in wages and in other items of cost. The President, in an effort to counteract this tendency, ordered that parity price be considered to mean parity prices less benefit payments, which interpretation would have permitted ceilings to be applied to many farm crops near the levels which prevailed at the end of the year. The will-o'-the-wisp concept of parity may be avoided by ceilings on the commodity at the processed level which will tend to hold down the price of the raw product. However, the law requires the processor's margin to be retained, thus introducing a further complicating factor into an already complex scheme.

Wages were to be regulated for the purpose of price control, but Congress gave the President no standards except that "so far as practicable stabilization shall be on the basis of the levels which existed on September 15." This is an enigma. The wages may be frozen as of September, or they may be permitted to go up to any extent to balance a cost-of-living increase from January 1, 1941 to May 9, 1942 (the "Little Steel" formula), or they may be adjusted to offset subsequent costs of living, or in accordance with some other policy. The language is very broad and permits increases "necessary to correct maladjustments or inequalities, to eliminate substandards of living, to correct gross inequalities, or to aid in the effective prosecution of the war." One could hardly believe that the measure, which conceivably covers such an important part of the price structure, was designed with the view of price control in mind.

COLD FACTS ABOUT WAGES [7]

Are the workers engaged in war production receiving exorbitant wages? Are the incomes derived from wages increasing out of proportion to other incomes? Are wages likely to throw our economy out of balance?

That all these things are happening, or are likely to happen, has been the burden of argument and peroration in the editorial pages and columns of our press and in the reports of many commentators and speakers on the radio. Most of this discussion has been based on the assumptions and evaluations of the commentators and writers themselves. Most of it has been without reference to the basic economic facts underlying our war economy.

What are the facts with regard to the wartime income of the American people and the wartime wages of our workers? Total consumer income in 1941 amounted to about $97 million. Total consumer income for 1942 is estimated at over $115 million. Measured on a per capita basis of our civilian population, this means that our consumer income in 1941 was $725 per person, and in 1942 it will average $885 per person.

When we examine the distribution of this income in detail, we find that in this year 1942 the incomes of millions of Americans were too small to provide them with food and other essentials to sustain their health and efficiency in the war effort.

The most recent government figures on income distribution show that 5.7 per cent of American households, or 2,242,000 households, have incomes of less than $500 per year, averaging only $324.

The lowest one-third of all households have incomes of less than $1335 per year. There are 14,200,000 households in this group and their average income is only $837 per year. The lower two-thirds of all households receive incomes of less than $2340. This means that the average income of two-thirds of all households is about $1315 per year.

How do these income groups share in the total income? The official estimates we have cited show that 5.7 per cent of

[7] *American Federationist.* 49:4-5, 29. October, 1942.

us will receive only seven-tenths of one per cent of the total consumer income in 1942. The lowest one-third of us will receive only 10.7 per cent of the entire consumer income; and the lower two-thirds will receive only one-third of the total consumer income.

At the other end of the scale is the highest one-third, which consists of 14,200,000 households with incomes of $2340 and up. In this group the average income is $5186. The highest one-third will receive 66.3 per cent, or two-thirds of the income received by all consumers.

Those with incomes of over $10,000 will have average incomes of $24,470 per year. There are 994,000 households in this group. This income group, which comprises 2.3 per cent of all households, will receive 22 per cent of all consumer income.

These figures speak for themselves. They go to the heart of the cost of living problem because they determine how much families and individuals are able to buy of the available essentials of living. These figures are especially important when we consider that low income families spend every cent of their income and sometimes spend more than their income for the essential living expenses—food, shelter and clothing. Families with incomes of less than $1000 normally spend more than 40 per cent of their income on food alone. Those whose incomes are in higher brackets are likely to spend much less for the essentials of living. Families whose incomes range from $5000 to $10,000 per year spend only 64 per cent for current consumption and those receiving incomes of $20,000 or more spend only 35.1 per cent.

Let us now consider wages paid to individuals. Most of us in America are wage-earners. To most of us wages or salaries received for work are the sole source of livelihood. The average wage income of all wage-earners is not a high income. According to the census of 1940, the average income from wages and salaries received in 1939 by wage and salary earners was $877.

In many parts of the country, the average wage income of all classes of workers was even lower. In Georgia the average was

$558, in Alabama $500 and in Mississippi it was $386. In terms of average weekly wage income this meant that in 1939 all wage workers throughout the country averaged only $16.87 per week and that in Mississippi their average wage income was only $7.32 per week.

This figure does not include income other than wages, such as income from farming, business, dividends and interest. However, according to the census, wage workers relied almost entirely on wages for their living. Five-sixths of the wage workers who received additional income from sources other than wages had a supplementary income which amounted to less than 96 cents per week, or less than $50 per year. Only one-sixth of all wage-earners received more than that amount in addition to their wages.

It is a common practice to refer to wages in manufacturing industries as if these wages represented wages and income levels of all American workers. As a matter of fact, less than one-third of all non-farm workers are employed in manufacturing. There are about 13.5 million workers employed in manufacturing industries as compared with our total civilian work force, outside agriculture, of 42 million persons. The reason we hear more about wages of factory workers is that payroll reporting in manufacturing industries is far more complete than in other branches of industry.

Since the outbreak of the war the share of wages in the national income has increased substantially. This increase, however, does not measure the increase in wage levels. It reflects primarily a great increase in employment. It is mainly the result of our drive to mobilize manpower for maximum production.

In the last two years employment has been rapidly gaining. Many more workers are receiving wages than before the war. In addition, work has become more intensive and hours of work have lengthened. A large number of workers employed long hours receive more because of overtime work without any substantial change in their hourly wage rates.

But, even so, the increases in the workers' earnings have not been by any means excessive. Even in manufacturing, where higher wage standards generally prevail, wage advances have been moderate.

According to Department of Labor figures, at the beginning of 1942 half the workers employed in manufacturing received wages of less than $30 per week and 24 per cent were receiving less than $20 per week. Considering the Department of Labor figure of $30.27 per week to be the minimum "maintenance" budget for a family of four, it is significant that half the American factory workers earned less than enough to support with their wages a family of four at a bare subsistence level.

Wages of workers in war industries were slightly higher. This was chiefly due to the proportionately greater number of skilled workers employed in war manufacturing plants than in civilian production. A further reason for the difference was the greater amount of overtime paid for longer work schedules in war plants. Whereas half the workers in war plants received less than $37 per week, half the workers in all manufacturing received less than $30 per week. Whereas in January, 1942, the average hourly earnings of all factory workers were 76 cents per hour, in war industries they were 84 cents per hour. On the basis of these latest available figures for war industries, it is clear that in general the wages of war workers were not substantially higher than the wages prevailing in all manufacturing industries.

During the first three war years, average hourly earnings, which include overtime, have risen substantially. But the purchasing power of these money earnings has been largely offset by rising prices. Between August, 1939, and July, 1942, average hourly earnings increased from 63.4 cents to 85 cents per hour. But real wages, adjusted for the rise in the cost of living, rose to only 72 cents, an increase of only 8.6 cents in the three-year period.

The weekly earnings of factory workers averaged $24.52 in August, 1939, and $38.52 in July, 1942. Here again the increase since August, 1939, reflected chiefly longer hours and the greatly increased burden of overtime work and here also the increases were largely offset by the increases in living costs.

Wage rates are schedules of pay established in proportion to the skill and aptitude of a particular worker on his job. A wage rate reflects a standard of compensation, but it is not a measure of pay received by the worker in terms of his performance and in terms of the stability of his job. Wage rates are not a measure of the worker's income. Stability of employment, hours of work, the amount of overtime paid and a number of other factors modify the value of a particular wage standard as a measure of the worker's income the year 'round.

For example, the average hourly earnings, which include wage rates plus overtime, of building and construction workers were about $1.16 per hour in July, 1942. These hourly earnings are better than the average and it is common to consider building trades workers as workers whose wages are in the higher brackets. But are they?

A junior stenographer employed by the government the year 'round at $1440 per year averages 61 cents per hour, or $27.10 per week for a 44-hour week. It would appear that the building worker's hourly pay is almost twice as high. In reality, the young woman's annual earnings are somewhat higher than the average annual earnings of building trades mechanics and laborers.

WEEKLY EARNINGS OF AMERICAN FACTORY WORKERS

Weekly Wage	*No. of Wage Earners*	*Standard of Living*
$50 and over	1,410,000	Comfort
$40 to $50	1,650,000	Minimum Decency
$30 to $40	2,240,000	Bare Subsistence
$20 to $30	2,810,000	Poverty
Under $20	2,490,000	

The building workers' jobs are seasonal. Even when construction is under way the work may often be interrupted by weather. A job seldom lasts more than a few weeks and there are spells of waiting and unemployment in between. To earn enough to live on the whole year, building workers must travel at their own expense from one locality to another. In contrast, even in industries in which hourly rates are below the average wage standard but where the work is steady, workers may often be found to receive higher annual compensation than construction mechanics and other skilled craftsmen whose employment is highly seasonal. Of course, in highly seasonal industries in which wage rates are low, as for example in canning, the annual income is far below the average standard.

Important disparities in our wage structure are not disparities resulting from excessive wages. They are disparities resulting from substandard wages paid in many occupations in which skill and performance justify higher pay.

Manpower mobilization for war cannot be accomplished solely by wage adjustments which make work on key jobs attractive.

But manpower mobilization cannot be accomplished equitably and effectively unless the glaring inequalities in pay for like work are eliminated.

Maximum production and maximum efficiency of workers cannot be attained by wage adjustments alone. But maximum production and maximum efficiency cannot be attained unless substandard wage income is brought at least to the level of minimum income necessary to maintain workers in good health and to give them the stamina and strength for the attainment of top production.

The War Labor Board formula, freezing wages at the January, 1941, levels adjusted for a 15 per cent rise in the cost of living, is not a workable stabilization formula. It is not designed to facilitate or speed the war effort. The real cost of living between January, 1941, and May, 1942, rose more than 15 per cent. In manufacturing industries hourly earnings rose 18 per cent during this time and wage rates rose about 15 per cent. These increases, however, have differed widely. In the case of the telephone and telegraph industry, for example, even the average hourly earnings, which include overtime pay, increased only 3 per cent. In electric light and power the increase was 7.3 per cent. In anthracite coal it was 7.1 per cent. In printing and publishing it was only 6 per cent, and in glass manufacturing it was 8.2 per cent.

A wage stabilization program which is effective must of necessity be flexible enough to eliminate wage disparities in the strategic sections of the wage structure.

It must be a program whose primary aim is to achieve stabilization which does not hold back but furthers war production.

OFFER WAGE PLAN FOR ELECTRICIANS [8]

The United Electrical, Radio and Machine Workers of America (C.I.O.), said to represent more than 450,000 war workers in the largest electrical plants, proposed a wage adjustment formula today to cover the entire electrical industry and designed to complement the War Labor Board's "Little Steel" formula.

The proposal, which was sent to James F. Byrnes, director of economic stabilization, and heads of other federal agencies, suggested that Mr. Byrnes convene spokesmen for his board, for the Office of Price Administration, the W.L.B., the Food Administration and the electrical industry to work out a new wage-cost of living plan.

As submitted for discussion by the conference, the program was set forth as follows:

1. The union will voluntarily abstain from damaging the cost of living wage rise that would be negotiated next month when our collective bargaining agreements are expiring.

2. Each firm will from March 15 to Aug. 15 of this year pay into a special fund an amount to cover the increase in cost of living from May 15, 1942, to March 15, 1943, for its employes covered by our collective bargaining agreements.

3. During the same period the government agencies will undertake to carry out their responsibilities to halt rising prices, to bring about a real rationing program, to organize food distribution properly, to enact a fair tax program and really to stabilize our war economy as they were directed to do nearly one year ago by the President of the United States in his "seven-point" economic program.

4. On Aug. 15 of this year the same representatives shall again convene.

5. If by that time the responsible government agencies have in fact fulfilled their obligations to the whole country by really stabilizing

[8] *New York Times.* p. 14. February 24, 1943.

our economy, then the money accumulated in the special funds shall be paid to the Treasury of the United States in exchange for war bonds, which bonds shall then be distributed to the employes, each receiving his equal share. The special funds shall then be discontinued. Thereafter, each firm shall pay in war bonds a flat cents-per-hour increase to cover the cost of living increase that has taken place from May 15 of last year to March 15 of this year.

6. If, on the contrary, Aug. 15 finds our national economy in the same state of disorganization as now, and finds our government agencies still unable to control the situation, then each firm will add a flat cents-per-hour raise to the base rates of pay, such increase to reflect the increase in cost of living that will have taken place from May 15, 1942, to Aug. 15, 1943—and in this event the increase will be paid in money, to enable the working men and women to maintain their production efficiency.

The proposal was announced at the union's local office by Albert J. Fitzgerald, national president; James J. Mattles, director of organization; Neil Brant, an international representative, and Russ Nixon, Washington representative. They declared that instead of piecemeal consideration of each plant's wage problem the formula suggested by them could be applied to 950 plants at one time.

They issued a statement declaring that President Roosevelt's seven-point anti-inflation program had not been successful, that skyrocketing prices had not been halted and that "instead of real rationing we have a flood of press releases, alibis, excuses, delays, everything except a real rationing program."

Instead of a tax program which will raise money to defray the cost of the war, they said:

"We have a tax program which is undermining submarginal incomes."

"In place of wage stabilization, we have the so-called 'Little Steel' formula of the War Labor Board," the statement added. "We see the agencies that are supposed to stabilize the entire economy interested in just one thing: freezing, not stabilizing wages."

EXCERPTS

The most fateful results of inflation derive from the fact that the rise of prices and wages which it causes occurs at different times and in different measure for various kinds of commodities and labor. Some classes of prices and wages rise more quickly and to a steeper level than others. Not merely inflation itself, but the unevenness of the thing works havoc. . . .

Neither is it possible to escape the detrimental effects of the time-lag between the rise of different prices and wages. Trade union policies are futile in this connection. As long as the war is going on, labor may succeed in obtaining, at least for some groups, wages which correspond to the rise of commodity prices, but sooner or later they will face the choice between a sharp decline in wages and the maintenance of high wage levels with long-lasting unemployment for millions. In the long run, inflation hurts the interests of all groups of labor, as of the middle classes.—*Ludwig von Mises, Austrian Economist. American Mercury. Jl. '42. p.* 67, 69.

While the W.L.B. has been talking constantly about "stabilizing" wages it has, in fact, been handing down an almost uninterrupted stream of wage increases. The few occasions on which it refuses an increase make the headlines because of their very rarity. This gives the public a misleading impression of what the W.L.B. is actually doing.

It is instructive to concentrate, for example, on one feature of these wage increase decisions that has attracted remarkably little attention. This is the almost unparalleled length of time by which these decisions are made retroactive. Let us, from recent decisions, take a few instances at random:

On March 1 [1943] the W.L.B. directed the John A. Roebling's Sons Company to grant an increase of 5½ cents per hour *retroactive to February* 15, 1942. Here is an increase affecting approximately 7,600 workers, retroactive for more than an entire year. The case is not exceptional. On February 6 the Board awarded a general wage increase of 5½ cents an hour to the employes of the Carbon Limestone Company of Hillsville, Pa. The increase was retroactive to April 1, 1942, or for a period of ten months. On Jan. 28, 1943, the Board ordered a wage increase of 5½ cents an hour to the employes of the Columbia Steel and Shafting Company at Pittsburgh, Pa., retroactive to

February 15, 1942. On January 23 the Board ordered a general wage increase of 5½ cents per hour to the employes of the National Supply Company's Carnegie, Pa., plant, retroactive to February 15, 1942. On January 14, 1943, the Board ordered a general wage increase of 5½ cents an hour to the United Steel Workers of America, C.I.O., in the case of six subsidiaries of the United States Steel Corporation, retroactive to February 15, 1942.

This list might be greatly enlarged. It raises some questions of the first importance concerning the Board's policies and competence. To what extent are these astonishingly long retroactive periods the result of the Board's own failure to decide wage questions at the time that they are brought before it? What is the effect upon a company's finances of having to pay retroactive wage advances for periods of a whole year? What is the effect on inflation of paying out retroactive advances for a full year in a lump sum to workers? What is the effect of these retroactive increases on workers whose cases have not yet been decided?—*Editorial. New York Times. Mr. 6, '43. p.* 12.

A WAGE CEILING

SOME MAJOR ASPECTS OF WAGE AND MANPOWER CONTROLS [1]

Economic science has been described as dismal, as using language beyond the understanding of the layman to draw attention to social evils but suggesting little by way of remedy, as being long on theory and short on practice. It appears, nevertheless, that economics is steadily becoming of more service in everyday life. In a book entitled *Dynamic Administration,* recently published in England, it is stated that Mr. John Maynard Keynes referred not long ago to the three great epochs of history described by the eminent American economist, Professor John R. Commons. First was the era of scarcity, which closed about the end of the fifteenth century. Second was the era of abundance dominated by the idea of laissez faire. Finally, says Mr. Keynes, "there has come the era of stabilization upon which we are now entering and in which the doctrine of laissez faire must be abandoned in favor of deliberate, conscious control of economic forces for the sake of the general social good."

This observation helps to explain the difference in the policies and techniques of government on the economic front as between this and the last war. There were a number of economists in government offices during World War I, but however much they tried to combat the laissez-faire doctrine it remained dominant. In general, governments followed the easy course of inflation in the conduct of the war. It seems to have been accepted as inevitable that with vast government buying on war account and the consequent increase in employment, earnings and spending, prices and wages were bound to rise

[1] From paper read at the Victory Institute on Industrial Relations of the National Association of Manufacturers, Edgewater Park, Miss., March 9, 1943, by Bryce M. Stewart, Staff of the Industrial Relations Counselors, Inc.; formerly Deputy Minister of Labour of the Canadian Government. 20p. typew.

rapidly, that there would be great waste of labor as workers shifted about in search of better paid employment under the urge of rising costs of living, and that the resultant increase in the cost of the war and the disastrous postwar consequences could not have been reduced.

War is an expediter of evolution in the field of the social sciences as in others; it telescopes decades of peacetime progress. Events on the economic front in the present conflict indicate that we are moving at a quickening pace into the era of stabilization and that the doctrine of laissez faire has lost much ground to the concept of control. This latter philosophy was voiced from time to time even before the last war. In his inaugural address of March 4, 1913, President Wilson said:

> There can be no equality of opportunity, the first essential in the body of politics, if men and women and children be not shielded in their lives, their very vitality, from the consequences of great industrial and social processes which they cannot alter, control or singly cope with.

Lloyd George said that England should be made fit for heroes to live in after the war. At Versailles an international labor code of nine points was written into the Treaty of Peace and an International Labor Organization, established as the agency to implement it in law and practice, made substantial progress. As examples in two fields of economic control, in the period between the wars central banking was improved and extended, as were also labor legislation and social security measures. Having set out upon this course, we are having our pace quickened by the present war. With its vast scale, its high degree of mechanization, its tremendous costs and its potentialities for serious postwar social conditions, governments are adopting one control device after another in an effort to harness the entire strength of the national economy to the war effort and to minimize for the sake of the general good the inefficiencies and injustices which the unrestrained operation of economic forces would bring during and after the conflict.

Any program of economic control will have the support of the public only if it is conceived and applied without fear or favor for the single purpose of the welfare of the whole population. If the increased purchasing power resulting from the war expenditures of government is to be siphoned off, the measures adopted must deal equitably with all groups. Wage and salary earners will not accept stabilization of their rates of pay if those who supply them with necessary goods and services are allowed to increase their prices. The proposition holds in the reverse situation. Stabilization policies, therefore, must include a number of controls such as heavier taxation and compulsory saving scaled to ability to pay and save, control of prices, rents, wage and salary rates and profits, control of the supply and distribution of commodities and services important from the standpoint of war strategy or necessary consumption, direction of industry so that it produces what is required where and when required, and control of manpower. This last must be exercised with due regard not only to the individual's maximum contribution to the prosecution of the war but also to his domestic and other responsibilities. In short, war-time control policies must embody the principle of equality of sacrifice.

Wage and manpower controls are among the most essential units in any battery of devices for economic stabilization in time of war. It is fitting that they should be considered together for they are closely related. Adjustments in wage rates are the most effective means of moving labor to desired locations. On the other hand, if by control of manpower a sufficient supply of workers can be made available at points of need, the upward pressure on wages that otherwise would occur is lessened. There must be tolerance in every phase of the economic stabilization policy for the requirements of other phases. For example, price control can greatly assist the manpower program. Price control can squeeze less essential industries and make plant, equipment and labor available for war production, and if prices are not held wages cannot be held. These considerations point to the need of vesting the planning and coordination of all phases of the stabilization policy in one central body.

Wage control is directed first to the reduction of civilian consumption during the war for such consumption must be reduced. The use of labor, materials, plant and financial resources must be diverted from the production of goods and services that civilians consume to those which the armed services expend in fighting the war. Reduction of consumption can be effected by resort to inflation or by a policy of control.

With the increase in the spendable income of the population in the form of higher earnings through full employment and overtime at punitive rates and with the decline in the supply of civilian goods as industry shifts to the production of war requirements, an increased demand is brought to bear on a diminished supply of goods. In the absence of controls a rise in prices begins, which is sustained throughout the war period, and consumption is reduced. Wages have to be increased to maintain the worker's standard of living; these increases force further advances in prices and the vicious spiral is in full operation. The inflationary process is simple; it calls for no courage in government and requires no enforcement. But it is unjust, since some groups are better able than others to adjust their incomes to the rising price level. It therefore allocates sacrifice in an arbitrary fashion and its injustices give rise to unrest that interferes with productive efficiency. It greatly increases the cost of the war, imposes a heavy burden of taxation and leaves in its train a serious problem of postwar readjustment. The greater degree of mechanization in this war forces the expenditure of a larger share of the national income on military requirements than in World War I and would necessitate a correspondingly greater measure of inflation to restrain consumption.

The alternative to inflation is the reduction of purchasing power by means of some of the devices previously mentioned and by the control of wage rates, which may be regarded as the keystone of the arch of economic stabilization policy in time of war. But control of wages is also an important factor in the effort to secure the best possible use of the labor force in war production. As the point of complete employment is approached by labor, employers increase wage rates to attract the workers necessary for extension of plant and greater output to meet heavy war commitments. In this competitive bidding the most profitable concerns and those with cost plus contracts have an advantage. They attract labor from other firms which may be producing essential products on which the very firms that are stealing the workers depend. Much production is lost in the shifting of employees and the recruiting and training of new workers. The national objective of war production in toto and in balance is defeated. The control of wages is a restraint on this wasteful shifting of labor, but a comprehensive, well-administered manpower policy is a necessary concomitant.

Canada has been in the war from the outset. The government looked forward to a long conflict involving costs beyond all precedent and realized that the national economy would be strained to the utmost. This view prompted the government to pioneer efforts in economic stabilization and especially with reference to the control of wages and manpower. The Canadian wage control plan was the first to be set in motion. Swollen payrolls, a mounting rate of labor turnover, and rapidly rising prices and wage rates, caused first by trade union pressure and later and in greater measure by employer bidding for workers, called for effective action. A partial control measure of limited coverage was adopted in December, 1940, but in 1941 the rise in living costs was double that of 1940 and a broad policy for the control of wages and salaries, mandatory on all private employers and their employees, was brought into force in November, 1941.

The salaries control order applies to employees above the rank of foreman or comparable rank. The salaries of such employees as of November 7, 1941, may not be increased without permission, but genuine promotions may be given to the established salary of the new position. Promotions to salaries in excess of $7,500 must be approved in advance. In the case of lower salaries the promotion must be reported within three months and be approved before the assessment of the employer's income tax return. A cost-of-living bonus of the same amount as that paid to wage earners, which is described later, may be paid on salaries of less than $3,000 but is not compulsory.

The Wages Control Order rules that rates in effect on November 15, 1941, are not to be decreased and may be raised only with permission and only if they are shown to be low in comparison with those for the same or similar jobs in the locality or a comparable locality. The order is applicable to employees whose rate of pay is less than $175 per month and to those on higher rates who are not above the rank of foreman or comparable rank. An employee is considered above the rank of foreman if his rate of pay is at least $250 per month, unless it is clearly evident that he is not above that rank.

When the overall mandatory order came into effect, some employers had been paying a cost-of-living bonus in conformity with a previous Order in Council. They were required to bring the bonus payment up to date and to adjust the amount of the bonus on all subsequent quarterly dates, as directed by the National War Labor Board. Employers who had not been paying a bonus were required to begin making payments in accordance with the order in the amounts to be announced quarterly by the board. The order provided that if an employer was financially unable to pay the required bonus he might be permitted to pay a smaller amount or not to pay at all.

The bonus is of two kinds—the flat bonus and the percentage bonus. The flat bonus, paid to all adult male employees and all others on weekly wage rates of $25 or more, is 25 cents per week for each 1 per cent rise in the cost of living. The percentage bonus applicable to men under twenty-one years of age whose weekly wage rates are below $25 and to all women receiving less than $25 per week is 1 per cent of their basic wage rates for each 1 per cent rise in the cost of living. If the cost of living rises five points in a quarter, the flat bonus is $1.25 per week, while an employee of the percentage-bonus group with a basic weekly wage rate of $20 will receive $1. If any employee works half of the full-time week he is allowed half the amount of the bonus, and no bonus is provided for overtime.

The base date for the bonus calculation is the date of the employer's last general increase in wages but in no case may be earlier than August, 1939, on the assumption that any such increase would have compensated for the rise in the cost of living from August, 1939, to the date of the increase. If evidence to the contrary is submitted, the employer may be required to calculate the bonus from some previous date but not earlier than August, 1939. The amount of the flat weekly bonus is to be reduced by 25 cents for each one-point decline in the cost of living, and if a wage rate is found to be higher than the rate generally prevailing for the occupation in the locality or in comparable localities, the cost-of-living bonus for the employees concerned may be deferred or reduced. The maximum weekly bonus is now $4.25, as a result of the 17 per cent rise in the cost of living in the period August, 1939, to October, 1942.

The War-time Wages Control Order is administered by the National War Labor Board and nine regional war labor boards, one for each province. Violation by any employer of the wages or salaries control order is punishable by fine and the amount of any salary, wage or bonus in excess of the amounts prescribed is disallowed as an abnormal expense under the Excess Profits and Income Tax Acts. Any person who in any way interferes with production with a view to forcing an employer to take action that would contravene the Wages Control Order or any direction of a War Labor Board is also subject to a fine.

Some reference to the wage control policy of the United States may be in order at this point. It is embodied in the President's wage stabilization order of October 3, 1942, the purpose of which is to stabilize prices and wages as of September 15, 1942. In effect, the policy establishes the so-called Little Steel formula of the National War Labor Board, which provides that if the average group wage rates for any establishment or bargaining unit have been increased by 15 per cent since January 1, 1941, to take account of the rise in the cost of living to May, 1942, they may not be further advanced. Where the increase has been less than 15 per cent, an adjustment to that level may be given on application to and approval of the War Labor Board. Increases in wage rates beyond the formula may be given only to correct maladjustments and inequities, to rectify substandard wages and for the effective prosecution of the war. If the policy is strictly applied, the inflationary force of mounting wage rates will be restrained, but much depends on the interpretation in practice of the terms, as "maladjustments," "inequities" and "substandard wages."

The formula in itself is generous. A very high base was established, for average money wage rates in the United States as of January 1, 1941, were at the highest point in history.

But the rates may be 15 per cent higher than they were at the base point to cover the rise in living costs of that percentage to May, 1942. This provision is liberal, especially for those in the higher wage brackets. The increase applies not only to that part of the regular full-time earnings spent in maintaining the individual's standard of living but also to the excess devoted to savings or other purposes. It is noteworthy that, while the cost of living rose 15 per cent in this period, average weekly factory earnings, according to the *Survey of Current Business,* increased from $27.74 in January, 1941, to $37.46 in May, 1942, a rise of 31 per cent. Any person employed forty hour per week, who received the 15 per cent increase recognized by the formula and who later in this period because of war production needs began to work four hours overtime each week at time and one-half, had his weekly earnings advanced by 32 per cent in this period of sixteen months. There must have been great numbers of such cases. One would think the formula might well have provided that, if the weekly earnings rose 15 per cent for a full-time week of not more than forty-eight hours, the wage rates would not be further advanced.

Acceptance of the position that a rise of 1 per cent in the cost of living justifies an advance of 1 per cent in wage rates, however high, sets an unfortunate precedent. The cost of living has increased during the last few months at an annual rate of 4 or 5 per cent, and there are insistent demands for wage increases. These demands are not for a flat sum sufficient to offset the higher cost of an adequate family budget. Generally, a straight percentage increase on the entire scale of occupational rates is asked. There are some demands for a flat $1 or $2 per day, which on weekly wage of $50 would mean a rise in earnings of 10 and 20 per cent, respectively, taking no account of the consequent higher payments for overtime. It appears that in anticipation of some rise in living costs despite the controls established a cost-of-living bonus after the Canadian pattern might well have been adopted. Under the system in Canada, employers are directed to give a bonus of a flat sum equal for all adult employees for every rise of one point in the cost of living. This procedure serves notice that percentage increases in wage rates will not be considered. It also has the advantage that the bonus is withdrawn as the cost of living declines, so that a better adjustment of wages to prices should be effected in the postwar period.

With respect to manpower policy, Great Britain has a more comprehensive and logical program than any other democratic country. She has, however, no formal wage control mechanism, but this deficiency is offset in part at least by other measures. The supply, distribution and rationing of the necessities of life are controlled by the government. People generally cannot buy as much as in peacetime, and the urge to press for higher wages is, therefore, restrained in some degree. Moreover, the danger of inflation has been attacked by the use of wage incentive systems or as the English say "payment by results." The employees earn more but they produce more. In manpower policy and its administration, Great Britain has set a high standard and has established a pattern that Canada, the United States and other countries are copying quite closely but with considerable lag.

The fundamental principle of Great Britain's policy is the placing of every able-bodied individual in that service in the armed forces, defense work or civilian employment in which he or she will contribute most to the war effort. After Dunkerque the British people awakened to the seriousness of their danger, and they have generally accepted the inconvenience, sacrifice and regimentation of their lives resulting from the mobilization of the nation's manpower in a spirit of co-operation with the government. The British people take the view that the government alone knows from day to day with the changing tides of war what is the most urgent work for each citizen and that the government must direct them accordingly. Many employees have worked sixty to seventy hours a week. These excessive hours have been reduced, and the average with overtime is now fifty-six hours a week. Men and women are moved from job to job and place to place as war production requirements necessitate. More than 8,000,000 employees in essential industries are subject to government regulations which prevent their leaving or being dismissed from their jobs without permission.

Out of 33,250,000 men and women between the ages of fourteen and sixty-five, about 25,000,000 are in full-time work for the nation in one capacity or another. In short, the policy is one of virtual conscription of the entire employable population. While compulsion may be exercised under legislation in practically every aspect of the program, it has been necessary to compel compliance in only a small percentage of the total cases. With almost full mobilization of the population attained, the government is looking to better working conditions and improvements in planning and managerial efficiency as the only remaining means of increasing productivity per worker.

The main features of Great Britain's manpower policy are: (1) war service for every employable individual who can be spared from his or her ordinary duties, (2) allocation of employable men and women to the armed forces, civil defense or civilian employment and direction to any job or area by the government under compulsion if necessary, (3) engagement of employees in essential industries only through the employment exchanges and prohibition of quitting and dismissal without permission, (4) penalties on employers for noncompliance with directions and on employees for absenteeism, habitual lateness and refusal to obey reasonable directions, (5) deferment from military service on the basis of the national importance of the worker's employment, regardless of occupation, though at first deferment was determined by age and occupation, (6) assignment of skilled workers to the armed forces only if they are required in their trade capacity, (7) subject to consideration of military strategy, the calling up of men for the armed services at a rate corresponding to that at which the necessary equipment can be made available, (8) training of workers in government training centers and private plants, (9) provision for the welfare of war workers in such matters as housing, lodging, canteens, day nurseries and travel and other allowances, (10) development of personnel management through government-assisted university courses in this field, (11) determination of manpower policy by the War Cabinet, and (12) administration of all phases of the policy by the Ministry of Labour, which operates through eleven regional offices with wide autonomy.

Canadian manpower policy is modeled on that of Great Britain but is less thoroughgoing. Its principal features are: (1) seven days' notice to the employment service by employers of their labor requirements, layoffs and discharges, (2) seven days' notice of termination of employment by employees, (3) restriction of offers of employment or of hirings by employers to persons having permits to seek employment issued by an employment office, (4) restriction of civilian employment of agricultural workers to work on the farm for all but sixty days in the year or longer with permission, (5) prohibition of advertising for workers by employers without permission, (6) authority to direct persons, in particular unemployed or partially employed persons, to accept suitable employment, (7) financial assistance to workers required to change their place of residence, advance of travel expense and provision of various supplementary allowances to workers directed to distant employment, (8) reinstatement of transferred workers in their former jobs, (9) prohibition of emigration to other countries without permission, (10) determination of manpower policy by the War Committee of the Cabinet, (11) administration of the policy for civilians and the calling up of men for military service by the Minister of Labour, and (12) decentralized administration through the regional offices of the employment service.

The Canadian program has a number of the features of the British policy but compulsion is not exercised in the same degree. In this respect Canada stands midway between Great Britain and the United States, for the American policy, nominally at least, is based on the principle of voluntary compliance. Its main points are: (1) compulsory service restricted to service in the armed forces, (2) control of employment through local, voluntary stabilization agreements, (3) deferment from military service decided by local draft boards which have a large measure of autonomy, (4) better utilization of the labor force by resort to the forty-eight-hour week and service to employers on such matters as absenteeism, high labor turnover, the greater use of women workers, production restrictions and stoppages, (5) determination of policy by the President on the advice of the War Manpower Commission, (6) administration of policy with respect to military service and civilian employment through Manpower Commission to whose jurisdiction National Selective Service and the United States Employment Service have been transferred though their activities have not been adequately controlled and co-ordinated as yet.

Patently, we have some distance to travel before we attain the British idea of war service for the whole people, by legal direction if necessary. Neither the United States nor Canada, for example, make war service for women compulsory. The United States, however, is exercising a considerable degree of indirect compulsion with respect to civilian labor. By the allocation of contracts to selected areas, transfers of workers to such areas may be forced. It was recently announced that workers of military age in specified occupations may be deferred from service in the armed forces only if they transfer to more urgent work. Deferments may also be cancelled. The President's order on the forty-eight-hour week is designed both to increase production and also to squeeze out labor surpluses and make them available for transfer. We may expect less reliance on the voluntary principle. Proposed legislation on absenteeism, the bill on National War Service and constant reference to the need for better control of industrial disputes evidence the trend of opinion in this direction. According to a press statement in the New York Times of March 6, Mr. Daniel J. Tobin, International President of the A.F.L. Teamsters Union, said that union members joining walkouts in defiance of their officers should be classed as enemies of the government. He pointed out, it is stated, that in England such persons would be placed in military service or if unfit they would be imprisoned. "Surely," he said, "it is a small price to pay in this dangerous world situation, to remain at work and keep the wheels rolling."

And now, some general observations on wage and manpower controls. There has been a good deal of criticism of the war labor boards here and in Canada because they have not maintained all wage rates unchanged. Surely this is asking too much. Before the war the wage structures of industry had many anomalies as between and within localities, industries and plants. The war tide of employment has brought the illogical and unjust features of salary and wage administration to the fore because many employees can now escape them by moving to better jobs. Wage control authorities cannot perpetuate these malpractices and can only reduce the resultant turnover of workers by doing what they can to rectify the basic conditions.

In normal times this country has several fairly well defined wage zones, but under present conditions these zones tend to extend their boundaries and even to merge as workers of a high wage area are moved to a lower wage zone to expand necessary war production there. It seems inevitable that during the war wage rates of a given occupation will gravitate first toward the higest rate for the occupation in the locality, next, toward the highest rate in the zone, and then toward the highest rate in any other zone to which transfer is not discouraged by reason of travel expense, higher living costs or other deterrents. Any wage control agency is confronted with these problems and must deal with them; it cannot say to an employer producing an essential commodity who has been paying relatively low wages that he cannot raise them. So many of the employees would take other jobs that the product, perhaps a key part for a new model tank, could not be delivered. Some would suggest as an alternative that the employees should be frozen to their jobs, but a regulation involving such injustice could not be enforced.

The first function of wage control is to maintain unchanged the highest rate in the zone for any occupation or to adjust it to rates in other zones only as necessary to prevent wasteful shifting of labor. The top rates in the high rate zones must be held as the anchorage of the national wage structure or the whole position will be adrift and beyond direction. The second function is to develop a positive policy for the progressive equalization of wage rates in each zone and between zones as necessary. This objective, of course, does not mean that the rate for an occupation shall be identical throughout the country but that the control authority should have its pattern of rates and the differentials between zones developed in advance and as cases are presented should render its decisions in accordance with the predetermined policy. If applications for wage adjustments are dealt with individually, one decision may give rise to a demand for a whole sequence of adjustments in other firms and illogical differentials will never be eradicated.

In the United States and Canada organized labor has opposed control of wages on the ground that it interferes with efforts to organize workers and with collective bargaining. These predictions have not been substantiated in Canada. The number of trade union members has risen rapidly in each year of the war and the number of new collective bargaining agreements filed with the Department of Labor in 1942 was greater than in any previous year. It may be more difficult to recruit members when the inducement of higher wages cannot be held out with the former assurance. The last war shows, however, that trade union growth sprung from the over-fertilized soil of inflationary wages soon wilts in the chill winds of postwar deflation.

In this matter of wage control, many employers are vulnerable for they have allowed their wage structures to develop with little rhyme or reason. The principal of equal pay for equal work has too often been ignored and such go-as-you-please procedures will not stand the stress of war. These employers vie with the unions in running to the War Labor Board for permission to pay higher wages. With many of them the basic problem is job analysis, evaluation and classification and the sooner they realize it, the better. To ease its own problem and reduce its load, the National War Labor Board should give employers all possible encouragement in this direction.

But one must not criticize employers unduly, especially while unions are protesting decisions of the War Labor Board and the United Mine Workers emphatically submitting a demand for an increase of $2 a day. This demand is a challenge not only to the wage control program but to the entire economic stabilization policy. A similar challenge was given by the United Steel Workers in Canada recently. After a strike in this basic war industry, the National War Labor Board of Canada rendered a decision increasing the minimum wage rates. While it is too early to say whether this action will mean a serious breach in the wage control bulwark against inflation, it has ominous implications. The issue in Canada as well as the United States is whether any pressure group can defy the government, especially in a time of national emergency on a policy established for the common good and in the best interests of the protesting minority itself. One result in Canada is that the National War Labor Board has been reorganized and now has more of the character of a court than of a board. This change may make it a more effective instrument of the policy, but time alone will tell.

The corollary to wage control policy is a manpower program that provides for the transfer of workers from less essential to more urgent employment, under compulsion if necessary. Employers will find a way to pay higher wages if the government presses for more production and if higher wages seem the only means of securing the necessary workers. The alternative is to give vital industries priority in the labor market and transfer the needed workers to them with proper allowances and safeguards.

The basic machinery for the administration of manpower policy is a well-organized, efficiently staffed, nationally administered public employment service. The British experience proves that conclusively. Here and in Canada we are far behind the British in this respect and for that reason our manpower programs will be less effectively administered.

The Canadian experience affords some indications of what economic stabilization policies can accomplish. From August, 1939, to December, 1942, the cost of living rose nearly 18 per cent. At the same point in the last war it had increased by about 40 per cent. In 1941 the rise was 7.5 points; in 1942 it was 3.4 points. The increase of about 17 per cent in the Canadian cost of living since the war began compares with 30 per cent in Great Britain, which has no formal wage control plan, and with about 20 per cent in the United States, a relatively high figure for this country in view of its shorter period at war. The time loss in Canada due to industrial disputes in relation to wage earners employed is about 40 per cent less in this war than in World War I. On the same basis the number of man days lost in 1942 was about one-third of the figure for 1917, the corresponding year of the last war. . . .

Results in the mobilization of manpower in Canada are also quite remarkable. Since the war began nonagricultural employment has increased by 50 per cent, employment in manufacturing by 100 per cent, farm production is at an all-time high and in addition 650,000 of a population of less than 12,000,000 have been placed in the armed services and a substantial proportion of them transported overseas. A great redistribution of labor has been effected as some industries have been expanded and others, less essential to the war, have been contracted. From November, 1940, to November, 1942, the number of employees engaged in the manufacturing of chemicals was increased 200 per cent, in iron and steel products 100 per cent and in steel shipbuilding and repairing 150 per cent. The squeezing-down process is apparent in several lines. During the year ended November, 1942, employment declined noticeably in highway construction, wholesale and retail trade, and in the manufacture of boots and shoes, furniture, pulp and paper products, printing and publishing, rubber products, hosiery and knit goods, musical instruments, edible animal and plant products, fur and fur products, heating appliances, and others.

In conclusion, much remains to be done by way of education on the nature of inflation so that these measures of control and how they operate for the good of every group will be better understood. Let each ask himself the question—"With my country fighting the most terrible war in history in far-away lands, on all the seas and in every sky, can I really expect to work no longer than usual and also to be better off when peace comes?" Those who have lived amid the horrors of this war know the answer. They understand that all-night air raid precaution duty after a hard day's work is dictated not by the government but the enemy. A woman war worker in England who had been transferred to a distant munitions factory was asked how she liked her job. Here reply was—"I don't like it at all but my man was taken prisoner in Libya and I want to get him home."

NEED OF STRONGER CONTROL MEASURES [2]

The War Labor Board continues to grant wage increases; and it is the rule rather than the exception to include in its awards an allowance for correcting inequalities, thereby fixing wages at higher figures than the formula of a 15 per cent advance since

[2] *National City Bank of New York.* (*Economic Conditions*). p. 112-13. October, 1942.

January 1, 1941, alone would support. This practice weakens hope for wage stabilization; for after every wage has its 15 per cent advance this reason—together with the provision for elimination of "sub-standard" wages—will remain to justify appeals for further increases. And how can "inequalities" be corrected, in the complex fabric of wage relationships, without creating fresh inequalities?

This country has been through three inflationary periods, all within the experience of men who are active today, and all consisting in simplest terms of a period of debt-making and distortion of economic relations, followed by crash, debt-paying and depression. A tabulation of changes in prices, wages and other significant elements in the three periods is shown herewith:

PRICES, WAGES IN THREE INFLATIONS

	Wages		*Prices*		*Cost*	*Farm*	*Indust.*
	Hourly	*Weekly*	*Non-Farm*	*Farm*	*of Living*	*Real Estate (l)*	*Stock Prices*
July 1914=100	(a)	(b)	(c)	(c)	(d)	(e)	(f)
July 1914	100	100	100	100	100	100	100
" 1915	101	101	103	100	100	100	128
" 1916	109	113	127	113	107	105	154
" 1917	126	129	181	189	127	114	162
" 1918	159	166	193	207	148	125	140
" 1919	180	184	202	230	167	136	196
" 1920	229	227	254	226	200	165	163
1923-1924=100	(g)	(g)	(c)	(c)	(h)	(e)	(f)
July 1925	101	100	103	113	102	96	130
" 1926	103	102	101	99	104	94	147
" 1927	105	102	95	98	103	90	172
" 1928	105	104	96	109	100	88	218
" 1929	107	107	95	108	100	88	299
Aug. 1939=100	(i)	(i)	(c)	(c)	(c)	(e)	(f)
Aug. 1939	100	100	100	100	100(k)	100	100
" 1940	105	106	103	110	100(k)	100	89
" 1941	118	129	115	141	106	101	93
" 1942	134(j)	157(j)	123	174	117	108	78

(a) Bureau Labor Statistics, annual average, non-agricultural; (b) N. Y. State, Manufacturing; (c) Bureau Labor Statistics; (d) Natl. Indust. Conference Board; (e) Dept. of Agriculture, March; (f) Standard Statistics; (g) Natl. Indust. Conference Board, Manufacturing; (h) Bureau Labor Statistics, June; (i) Bureau Labor Statistics, Manufacturing; (j) July; (k) September; (l) Value per acre.

The first period was the inflation of the last war, which was led by the great rise in commodity prices due to wartime demands and postwar reconstruction needs. This rise was accompanied, with a lag, by commensurate increases in wages, and by spectacular advances, later to prove ruinous, in real estate values, particularly of farm lands. In the subsequent crash the farmer's prices dropped, but wages and the prices of most of the things he bought remained relatively high; and most farmers who had incurred heavy debts to buy land at inflated prices were reduced to prostration. This was the source of the farm relief demands, which antedated the depression of the '30's and which persist to this day.

In the second period of inflation, in the late '20's, the farmer had small part. Nor did wage rates—although by 1927 or 1928 higher than at the 1920 peak—show extraordinary rises. This was essentially a financial inflation. The accompanying credit expansion was due to the stock market boom and to business and personal extravagance and over-borrowing, both here and abroad. Apart from the stock market the chief manifestation was in urban real estate development. The crash, starting in these areas, exposed the maladjustments dating from 1914 which the inflation had covered up. The resulting upset of price relationships and of international trade was of unexampled severity, engulfing the whole economy, not only of this country but of the world.

The third inflation is the one upon which the country has now entered. It is not duplicating either of the other inflations. Reflecting the concentration of government policy on control of prices, the overall commodity price advance and the rise in living costs so far have been less steep than during the last war. Stock market inflation is being escaped, chiefly no doubt because of the heavier taxes laid upon both corporations and individuals. Real estate values show little increase, in part because of rent controls and property taxes. Despite the high farm income, the experience of the '20's is still so vivid as to make another era of farm land speculation unlikely; in any event farm debts are being reduced, and the rise in land prices has been moderate.

The one area in which an inflationary rise greater than either during the last war or in the '20's is occurring is in wages. Since August 1939 the average hourly wage rate in the industries, according to the Bureau of Labor Statistics, has increased by 34 per cent, and the average weekly wage, reflecting longer hours and overtime rates, by 57 per cent. Precisely comparable data for the last war are not available, but an annual index of wage rates, compiled by the Bureau of Labor Statistics and included in our table, showed an increase of 26 per cent in the first three years of the war. The weekly wages earned by New York factory workers increased 29 per cent from July 1914 to July 1917.

A second area, in which the price advance has been almost as sharp as during the first three years of the last war, is in prices of farm products, up 74 per cent in this war as compared with 89 in the last. This rise started from a low level, as farm prices at the outbreak of the war were about one-third lower than in the '20's, and lower even than in 1914. They are only now recovering to the 1926 level. The advance in wage rates, on the other hand, started from an all-time high. Weekly wages are 214 per cent higher than in 1914 and 47 per cent higher than in 1926, and the work-week is shorter.

This brief examination of the main characteristics of the three periods shows that no two have been alike. The fundamental condition of inflation, which is a great increase in income and expenditure financed by expansion of credit, has been present in each case. Great rises in prices, in one area or another, are common to all. But the resulting inflations have not appeared in the same areas, nor have they behaved alike.

The first lesson, therefore, is that inflations do not exactly repeat themselves. They may be controlled by circumstances or government action in some areas, only to break out in others. The only safe control will include control of the cause, by absorbing the excess income.

The second lesson is that inflation has unequal effects in different parts of the economy and that it produces great distortions in economic relations. These distortions constitute the real catastrophe of inflation. If all prices, costs and values went up and came down together, in the same relations, the ability to carry on the exchange of goods and services would not be impaired. All business is made up of this exchange, and the fundamental requirement for conducting it is that costs and prices shall be in fair and equitable relation, so that each producer can buy the products of the others. Inflation violently disrupts these relationships.

The rise of wages causes concern because it creates such distortions. Organized labor, workers in the war industries, and farm labor are receiving great increases. In many other industries and occupations the increase has been small. This is especially true in the white collar occupations. The chart below gives the course of wages since August 1939 for certain groups among which insurance and retail trade typify the white collar workers. The data are those collected by the Bureau of Labor Statistics. The increasing spread between the various wage rates is a danger, for its creates inequities in the terms of exchange between various workers.

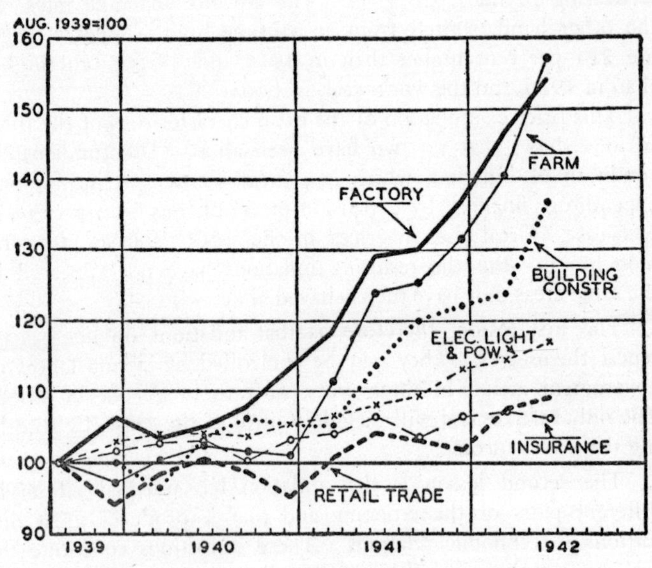

WEEKLY WAGE EARNINGS, WORLD WAR II
(Source: Bureau of Labor Statistics)

As long as the war lasts these wage distortions may not seem important. The Government is buying much of the product of the highest paid workers, and under war conditions high costs will not stop production. The great question concerns the situation after the war. Naturally labor is as reluctant to mark wages down as it is anxious to mark them up. Will the rest of the people be able to pay the rise in wages the government is now paying? Or will they be unable to buy the goods produced at such cost? Can the products of such highly paid workers be sold abroad? These are the sobering questions prompted by the inflation distortions, and by the showing on the record that wage rates established in booms have generally been rigid, resisting adjustment in subsequent depressions.

The third lesson from experience is that those who seem to benefit from inflation, as owners of commodities or land, or speculators in securities or property, in fact suffer most in the ensuing catastrophe—unless of course they cash in their temporary gains and pay off their debts. Not many do that, and stop there. This should warn the groups which are trying to get more and more for themselves that for the long run they are imperiling their own security, even without regard for the others they will bring down with them in the crash.

. . . Congress is formulating new legislation, requested by the President, intended to strengthen control over farm prices and to give the President more clear-cut powers over wages and salaries. . . . Provisions already agreed upon, however, show that while in some cases the Act will permit farm price ceilings to be imposed at lower levels than the existing Price Control Act, in others—notably livestock—the permissible ceilings may be higher. At the same time it will raise the "floor" provided by government loans on staple farm commodities, by requiring loans to be made hereafter at 90 instead of 85 per cent of the calculated "parity price."

Thus the new measure in some respects is less effective than the present Act would be if all the ceilings permitted were established. It will allow all price advances to September 15 to stand, irrespective of previous ceiling provisions or the relation of prices to parity. It will allow prices on the average to move substantially above parity before ceiling provisions come fully into play. And of course the measure will be even less effective if it includes an upward revision in the calculated parity, for which the farm bloc has been contending.

Provisions for wage control are less definite, since the authority is given into the President's hands. Evidently, however, the War Labor Board's formula—allowing a 15 per cent wage increase over January 1941 to compensate for higher living costs, plus additional increases as necessary to correct inequalities and eliminate sub-standard wages—will be the guide. Because of the loopholes, plus the uncertainty whether further raises will be allowed in case of future increase in living costs, the sufficiency of this formula to stabilize wages is still to be demonstrated. Employment already exceeds the normal labor supply; workers must be recruited among people who do not usually work for a wage; and the competition for labor results in "upgrading" and other indirect as well as direct wage increases, to dissuade workers from moving on to other industries and plants. In short, rising wage trends have acquired a momentum which makes more lamentable the failure to undertake wage stabilization earlier and more firmly.

The controversy over the new bill, which has centered on farm demands for an upward revision of the parity price, is a fresh climax in what is essentially a conflict between farmers and factory workers. For some twenty years the case for farm relief has been based on claims of disparity between the positions of the two groups. When farm prices dropped after 1920, wage rates, relatively, did not; and despite the rise in farm prices during the past two years the farm price-wage disparity, measured in terms of relations before the First World War, has never been wider than now. It is shown by the top and bottom lines of the next chart, which diagrams the relative changes since 1914.

The high industrial wages make for resentment and friction, provoking disunity at a time when unity is essential. They are drawing labor from the farms to the industries, although food shortages are threatening and farm labor was never more needed. They have forced rapid increases in farm wages, but without solving the problem of providing more workers. This explains the unwillingness of farm bloc representatives to submit farm prices to definite freezing without providing for adjustment to future increases in farm wages.

ANNUAL AVERAGE FARM INCOME PER CAPITA, FACTORY WEEKLY WAGES, NON-AGRICULTURAL HOURLY WAGES, AND FARM PRODUCTS PRICES

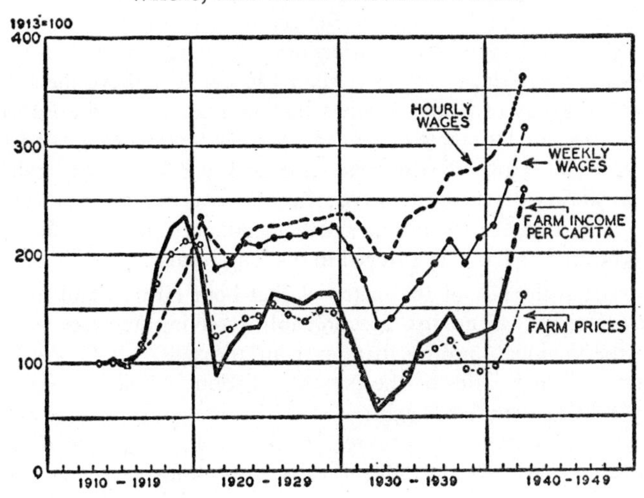

1942 plottings are latest monthly figures available, except farm income which is estimated for the year. Sources: Department of Agriculture, National Industrial Conference Board, and Bureau of Labor Statistics.

Representations such as the foregoing, however, do not cover all aspects of the situation. The supply of farm labor in last analysis will have to be augmented not by the attraction of higher farm wages, but through community effort and government policy. Farm wage increases can be countered by other employers, and competitive bidding for a limited labor supply is the essence of inflation. As for the farm-labor disparity, comparison between prices of farm products and industrial wages, on which the farm case is often based, is a comparison of unlike things. Wages are but one factor in prices, and prices of things farmers buy are relatively lower than the wages entering into their cost, because of the great increase in man-hour productivity in the industries over the years. Similarly, farm income per capita is higher than prices of farm products, because of the increase in the productivity of the farmer.

The chart also shows net farm income per capita, as computed by the U. S. Department of Agriculture. Its higher position, as related to the weekly wages of factory workers, throws a different light on the farm-factory relationship. In 1942 net farm income per capita is estimated at more than 150 per cent above the 1914 figure. Prices of things farmers buy, as reported by the Bureau of Agricultural Economics, are only 52 per cent above a 1910-14 base. The farmer is still at an income disparity with the industrial worker, relative to 1914; but he nevertheless has much the largest per capita income, both in dollars and in purchasing power, that he has ever enjoyed in his long history.

The plain fact of the matter is that both farmers and industrial workers, as groups, are probably receiving a greater share of the national income than ever in the past. Both are the seeming beneficiaries of the present inflation; its victims, on the other hand, who are caught by the rise in living costs as farm prices and wages advance, are the white collar and professional workers, charitable and philanthropic institutions, pensioners and other people with fixed incomes, unorganized labor, small business men, and all others whose taxes and living costs have risen more than their incomes.

Farmers and industrial workers are also the most numerous and dominant groups in the economy of this country. The record of past inflations shows that neither will benefit from a continuation of the inflationary spiral. On the contrary, they are inviting catastrophe for themselves, and for many other people. In their preferred position should be found a basis for a firm stabilization of the money returns of both. The answer to the demands of the farmer is a firm handling of the demands of labor, and community effort to enlarge the supply of farm workers; the answer to the demands of labor is the firm stabilization of farm prices. Both are needed. Over all is the basic need to deal with the causes of the inflation, by absorbing back into the treasury more of the income the government is disbursing.

A GENERAL WAGE CEILING [3]

One of the principal issues in the current discussion upon the advisability of establishing a general price ceiling for the purpose of curbing inflationary tendencies in our economy is whether or not wages should be included in the ceiling. Bernard Baruch, chairman of the War Industries Board of World War I, argues that if the price-ceiling method of preventing inflation is to be employed successfully, a universal price ceiling including wages is necessary. Leon Henderson, present price administrator, contends that a partial ceiling placed on a substantial number of strategic commodities, but excluding labor, would suffice to stop further price rises.

This paper attempts to strip the issue of all political implications and to demonstrate the economic wisdom of including wages in a general price ceiling. At the same time it is granted that other methods for the control of inflation, particularly increased taxation, are undoubtedly much more effective and should be employed along with a general price ceiling.

Inflationary forces at work in our economy are being driven on by the rapidly mounting volume of purchasing power which our armament boom is generating. Not only is the quantity of money available for consumer purchases rapidly growing, but the velocity of turnover of the greater supply is also increasing, thus further augmenting the quantity of "effective money." At the same time that it pours new purchasing power into the American economy, however, our armament program gradually is curtailing the supply of consumer goods available for purchase. Rising prices, therefore, are merely the outcome of a process in which buyers, armed with increased purchasing power, bid for a contracting supply of consumer goods. For the avoidance of further price rises, therefore, it is necessary to put an end to the spiralling of purchasing power, and at the same time to exhaust every means for preventing additional unnecessary decreases in the supply of consumer goods. Admittedly very little can be done in the latter direction. In the absence of steps designed to drain off purchasing power already in the hands of consumers,

[3] By James J. O'Leary, Wesleyan University. *Southern Economic Journal.* 9:24-32. July, 1942.

or to shut off a further expansion of purchasing power, the fixing of a general price ceiling will result in a hidden inflation, i.e., rationing of goods.

The establishment of a general ceiling on wages, as part of a universal price ceiling, offers one very important way to prevent further increases in the purchasing power available to labor. Inasmuch as it is the laboring class which is primarily responsible for the keen bidding for a scarcer supply of consumer goods, much can be accomplished in the direction of dampening down labor's growing demand for goods if new hourly wage increases are not allowed. It is granted that labor as a group may still find its purchasing power augmented as a result of the fact that hitherto unemployed workers with unsatisfied desires become employed and already employed men work longer hours.

A strong argument for a ceiling on wages, if a general price ceiling on commodities is adopted, is that wage payments are merely the prices placed on labor and are thus part of the general price structure. In our economy there is a rather delicately balanced interconnected network of prices—prices of finished goods, raw materials, and factors of production. Wage rates are ordinarily thought of as costs of production, but nevertheless they are prices for the labor factor which is employed in the productive process. As a matter of fact, wages represent a very significant part of our price structure inasmuch as wage costs very often constitute one of the most important costs of the business entrepreneur. In view of the position of wages in our structure of prices, it seems that to fix a general price ceiling, at the same time permitting further wage increases, would lead inevitably to a situation in which there would be generated an explosive upward push on the general price ceiling. It would seem that as a result the price administrator would be forced to allow higher price ceilings if the armament program were to continue under private initiative. Otherwise, rising costs would tend to wipe out industrial profits and thus discourage the production of armaments. It is true, of course, that there might be a successful resort to government operation of armament factories, any losses being financed out of increased taxation.

Another development which would probably grow out of a rigidly enforced general price ceiling, excluding wages, would be the development of a "black bourse" in which commodities would sell above the ceiling prices. A general price ceiling, furthermore, which allowed wage increases would necessarily lead to widespread rationing of consumer goods because of the fact that the pricing system would no longer be able to exercise its function of distributing scarce goods, i.e., it would be unable to offset by means of price rises the increased purchasing power in consumers' hands. The outcome would be that rationing would be required to prevent the quick exhaustion of a scarce supply of goods by consumers armed with an ever expanding quantity of purchasing power.

One of the more frequently advanced arguments offered against a wage ceiling is that it would result in a gross injustice to labor. It has been often stated that during the boom phase of any business cycle, money wages tend to rise more slowly than the prices of goods purchased by labor, thus causing a decline in real wages. Utilizing this idea, many are of the opinion that to place a ceiling on wages at the present time would be unfair to labor because during the armament boom real wages have been falling.

TABLE I

HOURLY WAGE RATES, ALL MANUFACTURING INDUSTRIES COMBINED

(Figures collected from *Monthly Labor Review*)

	cents		cents
1939—Jan.	65.1	1940—June	67.2
Feb.	64.9	July	66.7
Mar.	65.1	Aug.	66.7
Apr.	64.8	Sept.	67.1
May	64.9	Oct.	67.3
June	64.8	Nov.	67.8
July	64.3	Dec.	68.3
Aug.	63.4		
Sept.	63.5	1941—Jan.	68.9
Oct.	64.5	Feb.	69.2
Nov.	65.3	Mar.	69.7
Dec.	66.2	Apr.	70.8
1940—Jan.	66.3	May	72.6
Feb.	66.3	June	73.8
Mar.	66.5	July	74.3
Apr.	66.5	Aug.	74.5
May	66.9	Sept.	75.8

A glance at Tables I-V and Chart I shows that the reverse has been true. Table II reveals that money wages have increased from 98.0 in August, 1939, to 117.2 in September, 1941, whereas Table IV shows that the cost of living has jumped from 101.1 in September, 1939, to 108.7 in September, 1941. During the same period, therefore, real wages increased from 97.0 to 107.8. It appears evident that thus far our armament boom has caused a substantial rise in real wages rather than a fall. In terms of the orthodox marginal productivity theory of wages this phenomenon seems unexplainable. The answer lies primarily in the fact that the armament boom developed in an economy where there were idle plant facilities and unemployed labor. In other words, many factories were operating in a stage of falling average costs. It was possible, therefore, to hire more laborers and to pay them increasingly higher wages without raising prices because higher variable costs were offset by a greater decline in fixed costs as the plants moved to more nearly the best point of operation in terms of average costs. In addition to reductions in average costs with improved utilization of existing operating capacity, the increased demand occasioned by the armament program enabled many plants in decreasing cost industries to expand their plant capacity and thus to lower their entire average cost curve.

TABLE II

INDEX OF MONEY RATES, ALL MANUFACTURING INDUSTRIES COMBINED, 1939=100

(Index derived from Table I)

Month	Index	Month	Index
1939—Jan.	100.6	1940—June	103.9
Feb.	100.3	July	103.1
Mar.	100.6	Aug.	103.1
Apr.	100.2	Sept.	103.7
May	100.3	Oct.	104.0
June	100.2	Nov.	104.8
July	99.4	Dec.	105.6
Aug.	98.0	1941—Jan.	106.5
Sept.	98.1	Feb.	107.0
Oct.	99.7	Mar.	107.7
Nov.	100.9	Apr.	109.4
Dec.	102.3	May	112.2
1940—Jan.	102.5	June	114.1
Feb.	102.5	July	114.8
Mar.	102.8	Aug.	115.2
Apr.	102.8	Sept.	117.2
May	103.4		

CHART I.

INDICES OF MONEY WAGES, REAL WAGES, EMPLOYMENT, PAY ROLLS AND AVERAGE WEEKLY EARNINGS, ALL MANUFACTURING INDUSTRIES COMBINED

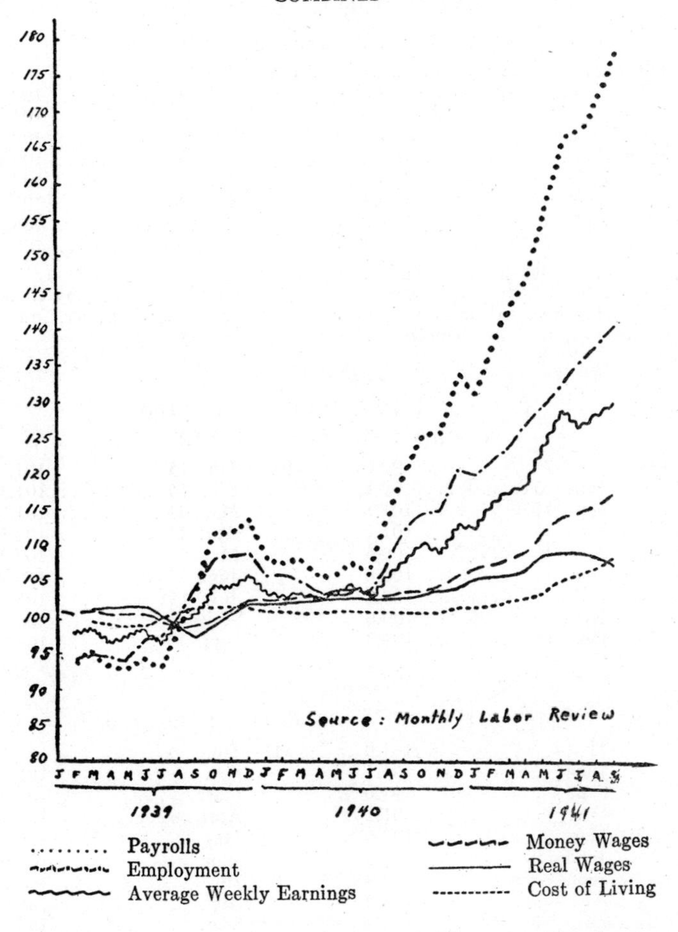

Whatever the cause for the rise in real wages, the fact remains that it has occurred. Opponents of a general wage ceiling might argue that if living costs have not advanced more

sharply than money wages, and if as a result real wages have been rising, why would it not be sound policy to permit further increases in money wages? The answer lies in the real wage figures for the period May-September, 1941. They show that

TABLE III

COST OF LIVING INDEX, 1935-1939=100

Date	Index	Date	Index
1939—Mar. 15	99.1	1941—Jan. 15	100.7
June 15	98.6	Feb. 15	100.8
Sept. 15	100.6	Mar. 15	101.2
Dec. 15	99.6	Apr. 15	102.2
1940—Mar. 15	99.8	May 15	102.9
June 15	100.5	June 15	104.6
Sept. 15	100.4	July 15	105.2
Nov. 15	100.1	Aug. 15	106.0
Dec. 15	100.7	Sept. 15	108.1

Figures taken from *Monthly Labor Review.* The figures are for goods purchased by wage earners and lower-salaried workers in 34 cities. The items included are food, clothing, rent, fuel, electricity, ice, house furnishings, and miscellaneous.

TABLE IV

COST OF LIVING INDEX, 1939=100

(Figures derived from Table III.)

Date	Index	Date	Index
1939—Mar. 15	99.6	1941—Jan. 15	101.2
June 15	99.1	Feb. 15	101.3
Sept. 15	101.1	Mar. 15	101.7
Dec. 15	101.1	Apr. 15	102.7
1940—Mar. 15	100.3	May 15	103.4
June 15	101.0	June 15	105.1
Sept. 15	100.9	July 15	105.7
Nov. 15	100.6	Aug. 15	106.5
Dec. 15	101.2	Sept. 15	108.7

TABLE V

INDEX OF REAL WAGE RATES, 1939=100

Date	Index	Date	Index
1939—Mar.	101.0	1941—Jan.	105.2
June	101.1	Feb.	105.6
Sept.	97.0	Mar.	106.0
Dec.	101.2	Apr.	106.5
1940—Mar.	102.5	May	108.5
June	102.9	June	108.6
Sept.	102.8	July	108.7
Nov.	104.2	Aug.	108.2
Dec.	104.4	Sept.	107.8

This index is derived by dividing the money wage rate (Table II) by the cost of living (Table IV) for each month. It is not strictly accurate because the money wage rates are monthly averages whereas the cost of living figures are for the 15th of each month.

real wages have tended to level out, with a slight decline in the September figure below that of July and August. We have argued that under the armament boom to date the expanding demand for all commodities has enabled entrepreneurs to utilize their plant capacities to a fuller degree and thus to reduce average fixed costs. Despite substantial increases in average variable costs, i.e., labor and raw materials, there was nevertheless a decline in average total costs because of the fact that fixed costs fell more sharply than variable costs rose. The real wage figures for May-September, 1941, indicate that manufacturers have exhausted the possibilities of lowering average costs through a better utilization of plant capacity. The outcome is that new increases in money wages are causing higher average costs and are being reflected in higher prices, with a resultant halt in the rise of real wages. It can be seen, therefore, that the possibility of expanding real wages through increased operating efficiency is largely closed. From now on successful demands for higher money wages are very likely to be offset by higher prices and lower real wages.

It may be argued that in a period of rapidly increasing profits (cf. Table VI) real wages should be allowed to grow to some degree out of such profits. Aside from the problem of how far we could go in this direction without destroying private initiative, there still remains the fundamental danger of increasing labor income during a period in which the supply of goods available for purchase is declining. If it is true that profits are growing too rapidly, the proper remedy for the purpose of curbing inflation is an increase in the excess profits tax, not the transfer to labor of parts of the profits.

It would seems that it is perfectly fair to labor to freeze wages at the present level as part of a general price ceiling. Real wages have risen substantially since August, 1939. In addition, Table VII and Chart I show clearly that labor has greatly benefited from the armament boom in the form of rapidly expanding employment, pay rolls and average weekly earnings. It seems quite apparent, therefore, that to place an immediate ceiling on wages as part of a general price ceiling would not cause an injustice to labor.

TABLE VI

QUARTERLY PROFITS OF 200 LEADING CORPORATIONS
(1939 = 100)

Quarter	*Dollar volume of profits*	*Index of Profits, 1939=100*
Jan.—Mar., 1939	$203,011,000	81.2
Apr.—June, 1939	217,896,000	87.2
July—Sept., 1939	201,664,000	80.7
Oct.—Dec., 1939	376,915,000	150.9
Jan.—Mar., 1940	326,490,000	130.7
Apr.—June, 1940	305,513,000	122.3
July—Sept., 1940	253,323,000	101.4
Oct.—Dec., 1940	380,293,000	152.2
Jan.—Mar., 1941	383,221,000	153.4
Apr.—June, 1941	377,000,000	150.9

Figures on profits are net, i.e., after reserves for taxes and depreciation have been deducted. Source: National City Bank, New York.

Even if we were to concede, contrary to fact, that to fix wages at their present level would result in an injustice to labor, a strong argument can be offered to show that in the long run labor may suffer more from the failure to place a ceiling on wages than from the fact that the ceiling is fixed. This is true because the lack of a wage ceiling endangers the success of an otherwise general price ceiling. If unbridled wages caused the collapse of the general price ceiling, as it might easily so do, and thus brought about sharply rising prices, one class which would be penalized most would be labor. Because of the stickiness of money wage rates during a period of speedily rising prices, and because of lack of knowledge on the part of labor of measures to mitigate the catastrophic effects of inflation, it has always been true that labor has suffered most severely from inflation. If it is true, therefore, that unrestrained increases in money wages are likely to lead to spiralling prices, and if such a process causes great privation to labor, it would seem that labor would be far better off to make relatively small sacrifices now in the form of any possible injustices a general wage ceiling would occasion as part of a general price ceiling.

TABLE VII

INDICES OF FACTORY EMPLOYMENT, PAY ROLLS, AND AVERAGE WEEKLY EARNINGS, ALL MANUFACTURING INDUSTRIES COMBINED, 1939 = 100

Year and Month	*Employment*	*Pay rolls*	*Average Weekly Earnings*
1939—Jan.			
Feb.	94.3	93.6	97.6
Mar.	95.0	95.3	98.4
Apr.	94.8	93.0	96.7
May	93.7	92.5	97.0
June	97.0	94.8	98.4
July	97.3	92.5	96.2
Aug.	100.2	98.4	99.5
Sept.	104.2	102.8	100.3
Oct.	107.8	111.5	104.8
Nov.	108.0	111.5	104.6
Dec.	108.3	113.9	106.6
1940—Jan.	105.5	108.0	103.5
Feb.	105.5	107.3	102.3
Mar.	105.0	108.0	103.3
Apr.	103.6	105.8	102.8
May	103.0	105.7	103.2
June	103.5	107.5	104.7
July	103.6	106.1	102.5
Aug.	107.9	114.0	106.0
Sept.	112.0	120.7	107.7
Oct.	114.4	125.5	110.1
Nov.	115.0	125.8	109.3
Dec.	120.7	134.2	113.2
1941—Jan.	120.0	131.2	112.5
Feb.	122.4	139.1	116.0
Mar.	124.6	143.9	118.1
Apr.	127.4	147.7	118.4
May	130.0	158.0	124.8
June	132.9	166.8	129.0
July	135.7	167.5	126.6
Aug.	138.0	173.0	128.4
Sept.	140.4	178.2	130.0

Figures taken from the *Monthly Labor Review*. In this table the base year of 1923-1925 employed by the Bureau of Labor Statistics for employment and pay rolls has been changed to 1939.

It appears evident, in conclusion, that there are at least four important reasons why a ceiling on wages should be fixed immediately as part of a general price ceiling. They are as follows:

1. A ceiling on wages would offer a significant means of preventing further increases in purchasing power available to potential consumers during a period in which the supply of purchasing power has already outrun the decreasing supply of consumer goods.

2. A general price ceiling would be destroyed if wages were not included in it because of the importance of wages, the price of labor, in a closely knit national price structure.

3. A wage ceiling fixed immediately would not be likely to subject labor to any injustice because real wages at present are higher than they were at the outbreak of the war. The stage seems to have been reached, however, where further wage demands will result in lower real wages. In addition to an improved real wage, the armament boom has brought about a sharp increase in employment, payrolls, and average weekly earnings.

4. If unbridled wages increase the risk of inflation, in view of the drastic consequences to labor of an inflationary movement it should now be willing to endure any slight injustice which might be caused by a wage ceiling.

NEW WAGE DEMANDS [4]

The most important development in the business situation, and the chief way in which the inflationary trend now seems likely to be advanced, is the spread of demands for wage increases. Both the Congress of Industrial Organizations and the American Federation of Labor are in back of the movement, and have appealed to the President not to permit any curb on general wage increases unless the country is to be completely regimented, with special reference to drastic retail price controls, rationing, and higher taxes on profits. Demands have been made on many major industries. . . .

[4] *National City Bank of New York.* (*Economic Conditions*). p. 27-9. March, 1942.

Wage questions are difficult to deal with because opinions are strongly held and feelings are easily aroused. Wage workers are sincere in believing that most of their economic gains have come through higher wage rates, and they are not consciously seeking to weaken the economic situation, much less to impair the war effort. The propriety of increases in some groups and under some conditions, where they will facilitate shifting workers to war jobs, is generally agreed upon. The argument that higher wages will check production and trade, which is valid under peacetime conditions, does not apply to war work.

However, much more than the general deserts of labor or the ability of manufacturers to pay the increases is involved. There is a public interest in the question which should transcend that of any group. It is certainly in the interest of all groups that the cost of the war effort shall be as low as is consistent with fair returns for producers. It is in the general interest that the inflationary influences present in the war economy shall be held under the strongest possible restraint, and that moves tending to produce a vicious circle of price advances shall be avoided. Finally, it is greatly desirable that the postwar situation be considered.

The major argument for wage increases is based on the rising cost of living. This is an argument entitled to sympathetic consideration, for if money wages do not rise while the cost of living is going up the purchasing power and standard of living of workers will naturally decline. However, there are other elements in the problem. It is generally agreed that an effect of the war will be to reduce the standard of living of the people as a whole, for the production of goods for civilian consumption will decline, as already shown. Thus a demand for wage increases to keep abreast of the cost of living is equivalent to a demand that labor shall be exempt from the reduction in living standards enforced on other consumers, and shall have means to buy its accustomed amounts of goods. Of course these goods in some cases cannot be had at all, in others only by leaving less for other groups.

If the "real wage" of the workers now demanding increases had been depressed by the war there would be a stronger argument for obtaining a greater share of production. But that has not been the case. Wage increases were general through the industries in 1941, even before the cost of living had begun to rise much. . . . By June, 1941, the higher wage rates, together with somewhat longer hours of work, had produced an increase of 30 per cent in weekly money wages, and the rise has continued. After allowance for the rise in the cost of living, the "real weekly wage" for employed labor now stands some 25 per cent higher than at the outbreak of the war. In addition there was a further great gain to the labor group through the increase in employment, which in many cases has meant that more members of the family are working.

Since August the further rise in weekly wages has only about kept pace with the rise in the cost of living, so that the real wage has ceased to advance. This is the principal basis of the new demands. In summary, they are designed not only to protect workers from the general reduction in the standard of living, but to maintain a 25 per cent rise in real wages that has occurred since the war began.

Whether this claim is equitable is not the most important point to be considered. The chief point is that the operation of economic law will not permit any group of the population permanently to enjoy such an advantage over other groups. Either the rise in wages must force all prices and the money earnings of all groups up, which is inflation, or when the war is over and production is once more devoted to peacetime uses, other groups of the population will be unable to buy the products of the high priced labor. The outcome would be depression, taking away through unemployment what labor believed itself to be gaining through the higher wage rates.

It may be thought that opinions as to post-war conditions are not germane to the present situation, on the ground that adjustments can be made as necessary when that time comes. Naturally, however, labor is as reluctant to mark wages down as it is anxious to mark them up. The American Federation of Labor in its *Monthly Survey* for February argues for automatic wage increases each month by the same amount as the rise in the cost of living index. One of the several advantages claimed is that the cost of living adjustment becomes part of the regular wage instead of a bonus. From the viewpoint of maintaining flexibility in the wage-cost structure, this claimed "advantage" is obviously a drawback. Far too generally, the rule has been that wage advances granted in periods of prosperity have remained a rigid if not frozen element in subsequent periods of depression. They have kept prices of manufactured goods in the air while farm prices, which are more responsive to influences of supply and demand, came down; and the resulting disparities have disrupted trade and industry.

Wage earners dread inflation, and in asking automatic adjustment of wage rates to rising living costs should consider that this, in conjunction with the farm "parity price" would provide a perfect mechanism for facilitating the inflationary cycle. As the cost of living goes up wages go up, industrial prices go up, the calculated parity prices of the farmer go up, food prices go up, cost of living goes up, and so the cycle proceeds. Both labor and the farmer think they are acting only to protect their own "parities" and each is inclined to hold the other responsible for the start. In fact any point in the spiral is a starting point.

At the moment there is reason for hope, at least, that the inflationary spiral may be checked by a halt to the farm price advance. It is hardly to be doubted, however, that the movement will receive a fresh impetus if wages are generally attached to cost of living indexes.

A common argument is that the profits of employers have risen, and that they can pay higher wages without raising prices. This claim is regularly made in demands for wage increases, and has as regularly been disproved by experience, for profits vary widely, while wage increases through competition spread from those who might absorb them to those who cannot.

The evidence of the article on manufacturing corporation profits for 1941, appearing subsequently in this letter, is that the rise of profits ceased during the fourth quarter of that year. It also shows that the profits earned are not in cash, but in increased inventories and receivables. There is nearly universal agreement among experienced industrialists and investment analysts that profits after taxes in 1942, when taxes will be heavier, will be less than in 1941. If the argument is that the earnings before taxes provide the source from which higher wages can be paid, then it is apparent that it is really the Treasury which would pay the bulk of the increases. The loss to the Treasury would be serious, in view of the relative heaviness of taxes on employers and the lightness of taxes on wage earners.

All these points are revealing as to the essentially inflationary character of wage increases under present conditions. Mr. Leon Henderson will not be considered unfriendly to labor, in view of his many utterances in the past, but he has taken a strong stand against new demands, on the grounds we have given. He wrote a letter to the War Labor Board early in the past month cautioning against a general rise in labor costs because industry cannot absorb many more cost increases without passing them on and contributing to an inflation spiral. He followed this up on the 21st with a notable address before the National Farm Institute in Des Moines in which he opposed not only any general increase in wages but any increase in the price of farm products much above parity. He pointed out that the decreased output of consumers' goods and services must spell a decrease in the standard of living as a nation. He stated that the principal question was whether this decrease was to be shared equitably, and said:

In this situation, the principle of adjusting wages to the cost of living should, in my opinion, be limited to those workers who are really on a substandard level. The spread between the wages in this group and the wages of the better paid, better organized workers should be reduced. If wage increases are permitted according to bargaining power, this spread will be increased. The strong bargainers will hold their standard of living at the expense of the others and those others will suffer a double burden, getting an even smaller piece of a smaller pie.

Although there may be some question as to who will determine which workers are on a substandard level and by what criteria, Mr. Henderson has stated views upon which all may agree.

Broad questions of principle are involved when any group of the population demands a higher relative compensation. There were on the average in 1941, according to National Industrial Conference Board calculations based on Census data, 51,342,000 persons gainfully employed in the country. Of this total 13,198,000 were in the manufacturing industries, 12,188,000 in services including the armed forces, 10,271,000 in agriculture, 7,843,000 in trade, distribution and finance, and the remainder in construction, transportation, and smaller groups.

Nothing is more certain than that the 75 per cent of workers outside the manufacturing industrial group will suffer if costs and prices in the manufacturing industries are raised, and they will naturally take every step in their power to increase their own compensation proportionately. If they are successful, all costs and prices will be raised and no group will have any new advantage over any other group, but with the difference that the entire situation is inflated, the cost of the war effort is increased, and the post-war situation is made less stable, and more vulnerable to reaction. The question is where does the interest of the 13,198,000 lie—solely in their own group, or as part of the greater group which includes all workers?

WAGES AND PRICES IN ALL-OUT WAR [5]

What is needed is neither rigid wage-freezing nor a do-nothing attitude, but a general and positive wage policy which cares enough about avoiding inflation to do something about it, flexible in application, but not so flexible as to permit everything. The specifications would need to be worked out by a representative body and to be definite enough to afford a guide

[5] From article by John M. Clark, Professor of Economics, Columbia University. *Survey Graphic*. 31:85-6. February 1942.

to boards concerned in the settling of wage disputes. They must be based on a clear recognition of the factors in our present course which are bound to lead to a big and calamitous inflation unless we change them. This wage policy would need to be joined to a farm price policy in a way that would put an end to the futile race of each to get ahead of the other, or else costs of living and wages will chase one another endlessly.

Until the past summer, we were getting only enough more guns to give us "more butter" too. People got more dollars, spent them, and got, let us say, half their extra spending in the shape of more goods, the rest going into increased prices. We have passed with painful suddenness from this golden age to an all-out war economy which has as its goal the devotion to war of more than half the national output in the new fiscal year, and a drastic cutting down of all civilian products that stand in the way.

When President Roosevelt announced this to the country, thirty days after Pearl Harbor, he was telling us two things.

First, we must work and produce as never before. Second, we must do it without the usual reward for hard and productive labor—more comforts and enjoyments. We shall have less of these things, because we must produce weapons instead. President Roosevelt was telling us, in his message of January 6, that our national "standard of living" is going to be reduced, heavily. . . .

The existing wage situation consists of a series of disconnected bargains, nominally free, but actually made under pressure of the emergency, which works consistently upward. Government boards reflect and transmit that pressure. They may recognize the inflationary effects of increased wages but be unable to act on this knowledge in any single case, lacking an over-all policy to which the case may be referred.

This wage situation operates in connection with a farm price policy which has helped push farm prices up to approximately average "parity," giving farmers greatly increased buying power and raising the cost of living.

In the aggregate, wages have risen ahead of cost of living and kept well ahead. This is true in terms of hourly wage rates, and still more in terms of earnings. While no doubt considerable numbers have failed to keep up, they would hardly be helped by encouraging the stronger bargainers to get still farther ahead.

Workers have demanded and received increases beyond increased cost of living, where employers had earnings out of which such increases could be absorbed. This gives workers increased buying power while the goods for them to buy are being curtailed, which in turn bids up prices. Further, it creates differentials between industries which the workers who are left behind will try to iron out, and *their* employers may not be able to absorb the increases. (The railroad wage case is perhaps the most recent.) It may squeeze the high-cost producers in the same industry and so create pressure on prices.

Workers feel they have a right to wage increases to match any further increases in cost of living, which would mean (a) holding the gains they have made so far; or (b) even increasing them, since earnings rise faster than hourly wage rates, and it is in terms of hourly rates that wage adjustments would be made, if the matter were left to "free bargaining." (c) Wage demands of this sort will not wait for existing contracts to expire. (d) These further wage increases could not be absorbed, but would increase costs and thus push up prices. (e) When costs of living rise because goods are short, the idea that "standards of living" in general can be maintained by increasing money incomes as fast as cost of living rises is 100 per cent delusion. In the conditions we face, it would lead to a hopeless pursuit-race between wages and cost of living. The speed of the resulting inflation would be limited only by the frequency of the adjustments. One principal result would be to put the real necessities of life out of reach of the unfortunate folks who cannot increase their money incomes. The money incomes of all groups should enable them to buy the necessities the country can actually supply, and if not, they should be increased, and that increase should have right of way. But to swell them to cover imaginary outlays on comforts and conveniences which *are not going to be supplied,* is to court trouble for a purely mythical gain. That is what will happen if wages, already liberal, are raised by a cost-of-living factor applied to the whole wage. If we go through this empty motion, in deference to people's settled preconceptions, the useless money must be kept out of the goods-markets in some more effective way than by means of voluntary bond subscriptions.

Adjustments to rectify existing wage differentials, including those created by the present wage policy, would always be upward, and would also push prices up.

To sum up, this wage policy justifies any wage increases which would not directly and immediately push up the price of the product concerned, though it might create excess demand which would pull up prices in general. Many of these increases to date have been absorbed by the economies of capacity output, but these are now exhausted. Future wage increases will push up prices. Further, it justifies wage increases based on cost of living (and increasing earnings *more* than cost of living) even though these *would* push up prices, and price ceilings would have to give way to them; ironing out of differential, even though this would push up prices; a total farm-price-wage policy creating dollar income vastly in excess of possible supply of goods.

Such an inflationary pressure cannot be successfully combated by price ceilings alone. Mr. Henderson's shoulders are broad, but he cannot make two plus two equal five. If costs are increased by approved wage increases, O.P.A. could not successfully resist. General excess purchasing power cannot be sterilized by direct price controls alone without the impossible job of rationing pretty much everything. Voluntary sterilization of excess purchasing power by buying defense bonds would not accomplish enough.

If we get a representative and responsible labor policy board, which accepts among other things the duty of formulating a wage policy aimed to prevent destructive price inflation, its efforts in this direction will be condemned to futility from the start if they are based on a platform which accepts and sanctions what I have outlined as the actual wage policy, and ignores or disguises the inflationary forces it contains. Any hope of success must rest on a frank facing of these unpalatable facts and of the necessity of sacrifice, fairly shared among all the people.

This will not be easy. But our old world is gone—we hope temporarily—and in the new world that has taken its place there is one supreme quality: courage. Let us show it, and demand it of our leaders. Have we not been thinking too much of who has to be placated, and too little of what must be accomplished, if the threatened life of our nation is to be saved?

CEILINGS ON WAGES? [6]

American labor groups have been unanimously against the imposition of wage ceilings. Their main argument is that labor is not a commodity, and that it would be an infringement on human rights to bring the matter of wage rates under government control. They say they don't want to submit to that kind of regimentation. That is high-sounding argument, but if farmers and industrialists submit to price control, they too are giving up human rights. The masses of labor, the 30 million who are not organized, are not making unreasonable demands. A Gallup poll recently showed that 62 per cent of laborers were willing to have their wages kept where they are if prices of what they buy are also kept where they are.

As a matter of fact, nearly everybody else is regimented, whether he knows it or not. Industry is regimented through priorities, and the time is at hand when thousands of factories will be virtually put out of business because they can't get raw materials. That is an invasion of human rights too, if you want to consider it as such.

The farmer's prices represent his wage rates. The farmer cannot understand why his labor is not just as sacred as the labor of a man employed in a factory. He works just as hard, and his income depends on his labor with his hands. If the emergency created by the defense program requires the farmer to submit to limitation of the return he receives from his labor

[6] By Edward A. O'Neal, President, American Farm Bureau. *Rotarian*. 60: 16-17. January, 1942.

in growing wheat, then it would seem no more than fair that the man who grinds the wheat or bakes the flour into bread should also be required to submit to limitations on the wages he receives for his work.

Farmers can't understand how the government can keep the price of a commodity from soaring unless there is some way of limiting the cost of the labor that produces that commodity. Certainly any price authority, in fixing the maximum price for a commodity, must take into consideration the costs that enter into production. In nearly every industry, labor costs constitute the bulk of the cost of production, and if labor costs are allowed to rise to inflation levels, then the cost of the finished products will rise correspondingly. Under such conditions, how can such a price-control law prevent an inflation spiral?

If you allow wage increases to go on unchecked, you are sure to have prices follow each wage increase as day follows night. You will have a continuous game of leapfrog that will end in inflation, and in all probability labor will find that its higher wages will buy no more than the original wage bought before the leaping began. As Bernard M. Baruch said in his testimony on the bill: "The way to see that agriculture and labor do not lose out in the inflationary race with living costs is not to seek special advantage for agriculture and labor over the other contestants, but to prevent the race and adjust inequalities."

Mr. Baruch speaks out of his vast experience on the War Industries Board during the first World War, and there is no man in the United States who should be listened to with greater respect on these matters.

Agriculture is willing, not only for the national interest, but also for its own long-time interest, to forego any speculative returns that might come from unrestrained inflation of prices, and it believes that labor ought to do likewise. We agree, of course, that wage rates ought to be fair, and in the administration of any system of control we would insist that consideration should be given to increased cost of living and to wage rates that are unfair. Farmers believe in parity for themselves, and they believe in parity for the other fellow. They know that the nation cannot make the progress it is capable of making unless there is fair economic balance among groups.

There is another reason for avoiding inflation, and it is a reason that may be more important than all the others because it involves the future peace of the entire world. After the war the United States will be forced to assume the leadership of the democracies in world affairs. That means that it must trade with the other democracies, and it will not be able to trade with them on an inflated price level. If American prices for industrial goods and other products are so high that other nations cannot buy them, then world reconstruction will be simply a beautiful dream that will not come true. There is more at stake here than most people realize, but Americans simply must understand these things if their country is to win the peace.

America's abundance of food and fiber is a powerful weapon. It cannot be used with maximum effectiveness as a weapon if prices are inflated to unreasonable levels. Agricultural abundance may well prove to be the deciding factor in preserving freedom for this generation and for the generations to come.

Some people argue to the effect that if you keep agriculture, labor, and industry in a condition of economic balance, then it does not matter if the level of that balance is a high-price level or a low-price level. That is perhaps the most seductive of all arguments for inflation. The trouble with it is that it neglects entirely the millions of people who must live on fixed incomes. There are millions of federal, state, county, and municipal employees—policemen, firemen, public-school teachers, for example—widows living on annuities, old-age pensioners, plus armies of clerks and unorganized workers, and so on. Incredible hardships will be visited upon these groups if the general price level becomes inflated. It will endanger the actual value of millions of life-insurance policies and savings-bank accounts. "Except for human slaughter and maiming and all that goes with them," says Mr. Baruch, "inflation is the most destructive of the consequences of war."

A witches' brew of all the ingredients of inflation is already in the pot—rapidly increasing employment, advancing wages, a bigger national income than we have enjoyed for years, curtailment in production of consumers' goods, a policy of get-the-job-done-at-any-cost in the armament field, rapidly rising farm income, and a general tendency toward freer spending by individuals. The only thing that has prevented an inflation in the stock market is the fear of taxation. If the brakes are not applied, carefully and judiciously but firmly, it is almost certain that an inflationary spiral will develop very shortly. The only agency that can prevent it is the federal government and the federal government will probably be helpless without additional authority from Congress in the form of a price-control law that will really control.

If Congress passes a bill without teeth in it, one that leaves out of it one of the most dangerous factors in bringing about inflation, Congress will have to shoulder the responsibility for having failed to take drastic action in time to prevent the hurricane. In this time of national peril it will be unfortunate if there isn't enough statesmanship in Congress to place the national welfare above the pressure of the inflation bloc and a few favored groups by putting through a price-control measure that will really control.

UNIONS, WAGES AND INFLATION [7]

Sir: The following is an open letter that I have written, addressed to the leaders of organized labor.

To Messrs. William Green and Philip Murray: I am addressing this appeal to you because never before did the fate of America depend so much on the cool intelligence and the warm patriotism of you, the leaders of organized labor. Whether we emerge from this war a buoyant and optimistic people, ready to lay the foundations for a better and happier life, or whether we come out an embittered and sodden people,

[7] Letter by Harold Mager, Technical Assistant, Office of the Secretary, Treasury Department, Washington. *New Republic.* 107:285-7. September 7, 1942.

joyless even in victory, our political life poisoned and our hope gone, depends entirely upon you—and the millions of workers you represent. I tell you this because there are times when I believe you don't know your own capacity for doing good or harm; like the giant in the fable, your own overpowering strength. How then explain your attitude toward the great domestic crisis facing the nation today—inflation?

Your attitude has certainly not been one that recognizes labor's overwhelming role in the economy as a whole. If you had shown the proper understanding of labor's income in the scheme of the economy and recommended the steps necessary to immobilize a part of that income for the duration of the war, it would not have been necessary for the President to take the action to which he has just committed himself—wage stabilization. Cry as you will against the avarice and cupidity of the farm bloc who have exploited the nation in their own selfish interests. Cry out as you should against the Neanderthal-mentality of bloated plutocrats who won't be satisfied till they have foisted a sales tax on labor and have secured lower personal, corporate and excess profits taxes on themselves. Point out, if you will, that from 1940 to 1941, according to *The Survey of Current Business,* agricultural income increased by 40.9 per cent, the net income from incorporated business by 30.4 per cent, and compensation for employees by only 23 per cent. But when you have done all this, remember, please, that out of a total national income of $94,500,000,000 in 1941 agriculture received only $6,200,000,000, incorporated business $7,300,000,000, and salaried and non-salaried employees—$64,700,000,000. While business and the farmer may roar like lions, labor is not exactly a lamb.

These are the figures which have prompted the President's intervention. For while the farm bloc cried for higher prices for its own produce, it was inevitable that labor demand more for itself; and a policy of countering provocation with provocation is designed neither to win the war nor to stop inflation. Worse still, it is a policy for which labor, because of its preponderant share in the national income, would have to shoulder the burden of responsibility.

Given an economy that is producing at peak-level and which, for that reason, can expand its production of war goods only at the expense of civilian goods, is the President not justified, therefore, in demanding that a halt be put somewhere on the process of income-increase-by-mutual-provocation?

If I seem to labor a point that is obvious to a large section of the American people, it is only because your respective organizations have shown no inclination to meet it head-on in their so-called anti-inflation programs. I say "so-called" advisedly, for no program, whatever its other merits, is entitled to be treated seriously as a contribution to the struggle against inflation that ignores, or shoves to one side, the most important element making for inflation. In the nature of the circumstances, therefore, the issues you chose to raise, however meritorious in other respects—and I believe that every one of them deserves support—were destined to be treated cavalierly and pushed to one side. Instead of sponsoring a program predicated upon labor's overwhelming stake in the national income, a program designed to protect that stake whilst immobilizing the purchasing power that would be created, you chose to ignore, or make little of, that stake and to emphasize other causative factors, psychologically and morally of the greatest, but economically of the least, significance. It is simply a case of a plump, red apple, rotten in the inside, that has fooled no one but yourselves.

I have before me the July issue of *Labor's Monthly Survey,* organ of the A.F.L., and the August number of *Economic Outlook,* organ of the C.I.O., describing the official attitude of both your organizations on the subject of inflation. In spite of the excellent recommendations that are made, the programs as a whole are content to deal with matters that belong on the periphery, not at the heart, of a real honest-to-goodness anti-inflation campaign. Both programs advocate stricter price control, an equitable and democratic system of rationing of scarce commodities, and increased corporate and excess profits taxes. Although the A.F.L. program is content to ask simply for "progressive income taxation designed to prevent personal profiteering in war time," the C.I.O. comes out flatly for a

100 per cent tax on all salaries above $25,000 a year, higher estate and gift taxes, and mandatory joint returns. The A.F.L. program highlights wage adjustments through the process of collective bargaining, voluntary wage stabilization agreements, the formation of a Wage Policy Commission, even the payment of wage increases in war bonds; the C.I.O. program has nothing to say on these matters. Finally, the A.F.L. advocates the "purchase of war bonds by all citizens on the widest possible scale."

Yes, gentlemen, these proposals belong in any decent, sincere program to combat inflation. But do they, when you put them all together, add up to such a program? Will they effectively immobilize the billions of dollars in excess purchasing power which labor—and primarily labor—will receive from coming on the market and ultimately destroying the price structure, the cost structure, the wage structure, and, yes, even the moral structure that today hangs so precariously in the balance?

I repeat, you have chosen to ignore, or make little of, the importance of labor-income, sometimes misleading the public with half-truths. In these ways you have played into the hands of your enemies. This could never have happened if you openly admitted to the inflationary possibilities of labor-income in the present period and had a genuine program for drawing off the excess.

What have you gained by iterating and reiterating that wage *increases* in industries that are now enjoying huge wartime profits can be absorbed by the companies without causing increased prices and, for that reason, are without inflationary effect? The argument is a half-truth and when it becomes generally known as such, as inevitably it must, it acts as a boomerang. Don't you think that people today know that even though the producer need not put his price up, wage-earners, coming to market with the extra money they have earned, will exert an irresistible pressure—in spite of ceiling prices and even rationing—that must ultimately force the price up? By this sort of argument you succeed only in convincing people that labor is interested in one thing—to get all it can while the getting's good.

Or what can you gain from maintaining that wage *increases* cannot be responsible for inflationary pressures that exist since—I quote *Labor's Monthly Survey*—they will constitute "a much smaller part of the 1942 increase in national income than one-fifth?" Has anybody ever maintained that increased wages are solely responsible for the expansion in the national income? This is simply a case of setting up a straw man only to knock him down. But when it is pointed out to the people that wage increases plus the much more important addition to the income stream resulting from the absorption into industry of millions of America's formerly unemployed are primarily responsible for the expansion of the national income, isn't it labor, then, that gets knocked down?

Or is there a premium on irresponsibility that prompts labor to declare in the July issue of the *Survey* that it is false to declare that rising wages cause prices to rise, since in the period from 1929 to 1939 factory wages rose 19 per cent while wholesale prices of manufactured goods declined by 13 per cent? What inference would you have us draw from this line of argument, Mr. Green—that prices *now* will also go down? Or that talk of inflation is just a Frankenstein's monster hatched in a diabolical conspiracy to chop off the head of labor? Is this the type of special pleading designed to aid your cause?

Or is there any sense to the argument, so popular with many labor leaders, that labor is willing to contribute its all to the winning of the war provided its present standard of living is maintained? The United Steel Workers of America—your own union, Mr. Murray—produced voluminous data for the panel appointed by the War Labor Board, showing that steelworkers received an annual average wage of $1,926 in 1941 and that—according to standard budget studies prepared by the Heller Committee of the University of California—an annual wage of $2,567 was necessary in order to maintain a standard of "health and decency." Are we to be grateful, Mr. Murray, to the leaders of the United Steel Workers for not pressing for the full standard? And are you not really injuring the cause of those who have a legitimate claim for increased wages —the men and women whose wage is really substandard?

Silly special pleading of this kind has done labor no good and much harm. It is the sort of infantile Leftist patter one associates—in a different context, of course—with the Communists, not with the responsible leaders of American labor. It makes many enemies and no friends; and what is more to the point, it has gotten you nowhere. By crying for the moon, you have only jeopardized your chances of getting a little more of this earth. Labor like all the other classes in the community will have to make real sacrifices toward the winning of the war, and the sooner it owns up to the necessity for this the sooner the others can be brought around.

The stabilization of wages and farm prices, although necessary, will not be sufficient to stave off inflation in the months, perhaps years, to come. It has all the virtues and defects of price control. It will neither provide the government with a red cent to finance the war nor draw off a red cent from incomes that will continue to accumulate far in excess of the available supply of goods. If, for a time, what I have called the process of income-increase-by-mutual-provocation is held somewhat in abeyance, the fact is that the government will still be in dire need for non-inflationary funds and the inflationary pressures will persist.

Your troubles, in a word, are only beginning. Stabilization will whet further the voracious appetite of the enemy, and he won't be satisfied until he has put you in his capacious maw. Already there are increasingly disturbing signs of impatience and irritability on the other side. There is growing demand for the imposition of a steep sales tax, no less than 10 per cent —and you know what that means. And there is the strongest likelihood, unless you can forestall action with a better plan of your own, of a withholding tax, or taxation-at-the-source. Time—in the quaint phrase of the lawyer—is of the essence. The crisis is upon you, and brooks no delay.

What's to be done? In the first place, you will have to give up all the silly twaddle about labor not exerting a potentially inflationary force; and secondly, your organizations must unite on a common program to be submitted to Congress at the earliest possible moment. In addition to the various planks in your own respective programs which are not incompatible with wage stabilization, its central core should be a plan for compulsory savings, graduated in scale, commencing at something like 5 per cent on net incomes of $1,200 and rising steeply to $25,000, above which level all net income, save for the payment of taxes and debts, will have to be invested in war bonds. The bonds should be callable by the Treasury with the proviso that if the index of employment in the postwar period falls below a stated figure the bonds are to be repaid at the option of the holder. If the term "compulsory savings" doesn't strike your fancy, call it "deferred pay," and if that isn't good enough, "postwar credits." Whatever you call the scheme, remember, it will be infinitely preferable to any plan that Congress is now considering or to the situation that is likely to develop if the Treasury relies increasingly upon the banks. If you sponsor such a program, I am confident that Congress, and the country as a whole, will respond to it in the manner it deserves.

The sponsorship of such a program by you will be an act of the highest economic statesmanship. It is the only method by which consumption can be restricted in the measure that will be necessary without restricting income. And it is the only method by which the working man can protect himself against the miseries of a possible postwar deflation.

WAGE POLICY FOR THE WAR [8]

The New Republic has from the beginning of the war been opposed to a flat ceiling on wages, or to any universal wage "freezing" which would mean that wage increases were to be denied in all circumstances. On the other hand, it has favored what is called wage "stabilization"—meaning that increases should not be general and repeated, but should be exceptional and for specific good reasons. It has also held that the working out of this policy must be left to the regular and flexible

[8] Editorial. *New Republic*. 107:7-9. July 6, 1942.

machinery of collective bargaining and mediation, rather than being established by edict.

Why is this a good policy, and what does it imply? There is just one major objective—winning the war and the peace. Labor has at least as much at stake in this purpose as any other body of citizens. The object in view demands that the workers be adequately fed, clothed and housed; in good physical and emotional health. Wages below what might be called a minimum-of-efficiency standard will not support productive workers. Such wages are being paid in certain instances; to freeze them would perpetuate injustice, slack work and bad morale. Wherever it can be established that they exist, increases are in order. Even where wages were barely sufficient to maintain a minimum standard when the rates were set, a rise in the cost of living would render them too low. Therefore, wage increases parallel to an increase in the cost of living above the base period are also justified, at least in cases where the base represented an irreducible minimum. If the steelworkers can prove that their members cannot get enough to eat and wear because of price rises, they have a good case.

But how about the "inflationary gap," which is cited against wage increases? This is not, as Mr. Ruttenberg seems to think, a delusion of governmental economists. It is hard reality, and not to recognize its danger is a sign either of ignorance or willful blindness. It is already true, and will become increasingly true as the war goes on, that the total income of the consumers in the nation is increasing while the quantity of goods available for them to buy is decreasing. No matter what policy is adopted about wages and prices, the consumers will not get any more goods than there are. Somebody must sacrifice something that the money in his pocket would seem to entitle him to have. If the consumers try to spend the extra money, they will provide a powerful impulse to rising prices; if prices rise, the people with the most money will get the available goods, while those with the least will do without. Labor has a greater stake in preventing price inflation than anyone else in the community. A wage increase which stimulated it might temporarily enhance the prestige of unions but it would constitute selling out their members. Awarding labor generally more money with which to buy a decreasing total of goods will not supply labor with any more goods.

How does this conclusion fit with our belief that all labor must have enough money to provide at least a minimum standard of productivity? A little examination reveals that it fits pretty well. The main item in the minimum budget is food. There is no real scarcity of most food staples in the United States, and none is likely to develop. We have to go slow on sugar, and may have to do without coffee, tea and other items, but we need not starve ourselves. The next item is clothing, and we shall be able to buy enough clothing to keep ourselves warm; the industry is not hard pressed and there is enough of most materials, except possibly wool. Housing is seriously short, but denying people the money with which to pay rent is obviously not the solution. More housing must be provided, while rents are controlled. It is in the items bought increasingly as one gets more than enough for a minimum standard that most of the shortages are found—home furnishings, durable goods of many kinds, better qualities of clothing and houses.

The main sacrifice will have to be borne by those who ordinarily can afford more than a minimum standard. Labor leaders need only to look at their own incomes, taxes and prospects of purchasing to see that this is true. And many millions of wage-earners in the higher brackets will have to share that sacrifice. It cannot be admitted that when the nation devotes 50 to 60 per cent of its productive effort to making munitions rather than consumers' goods, no wage-earner need endure any privation, no matter how high his standard at the beginning of the period. Yet that is the tacit assumption behind the statement that during this total war *all* wages must be increased, simply because there has been an increase in the cost of living.

Mr. Ruttenberg argues that the real remedy is price control and rationing. That is necessary, of course, but it is almost certain to fail if there is too much purchasing power trying to buy a limited quantity of goods. Mr. Ruttenberg maintains that those workers with more than enough cash for their daily needs will voluntarily and from patriotic motives refrain from purchasing scarce articles, and instead invest it in government bonds. We do not doubt that this is true of many, perhaps even of a majority. The wage-earners may even be better in this respect than the rest of the population. But Mr. Ruttenberg, as a good trade unionist, knows that there is always an ignorant or misled or conscienceless minority ready to undermine the standards accepted by the community, unless it is restrained. He knows that minimum-wage laws, union discipline and union security are necessary. The patriotic and group-minded ought to be the first to insist that what they are willing to do be made a collective rule.

It would seem to us that the labor movement would serve its own best interests and those of the country if it stood on the following platform on the wage and inflation issue:

1. A stabilization of present wages by collective agreements, with increases for those now below a minimum level, and increases for those subsequently brought below that level by any rise in the cost of living. These agreements to be open to revision if the cost of living rises, say, 25 per cent.

2. An income tax that would yield the major part of the money necessary to finance the war. Such a program would not only leave little of war profits and be severe on high incomes, but would have to go down the scale far enough to take something from all incomes in excess of a minimum standard.

3. The difference between the tax yield and the war cost to be made up by government borrowings, not from banks but from real savings and incomes. This policy would necessitate, we believe, compulsory loans, levied at the same kind of progressive scale as the income tax.

Such a program would assure an equitable distribution of the burden. Nothing less will. Any general wage increases will get labor as a whole no more goods, but will discriminate in favor of the better paid workers and against the worse paid; in favor of the chiselers and against the conscientious and patriotic.

EXCERPTS

General and indiscriminate wage and price increases will not solve any of our real problems. They will not give us increased manpower. They will not give us increased production. They are advantageous to the groups that get them only so long as other groups can be kept from getting them. The apparent advantages obtained by the groups benefited will prove short-lived and illusory during the war and will bring retribution even on those groups when the war is over. Those who demand them are only demanding another depression—*James F. Byrnes, Economic Stabilization Director, in address February* 9, 1943. *Vital Speeches of the Day. Mr.* 1, '43. *p.* 306.

During the year 1941 labor felt the effect of rising prices and, observing the profits of expansion, was all set for demanding wage increases that would not only make up for the increase in cost of living during the last year but, in addition, assure labor against the hazard of an anticipated further increase in prices. Thus, for another reason, price rises were losing their stimulating effect on production and became less effective as a means for curtailing consumption when the "spiral" pushed up prices and wages in mutual causation.

Rising wages had a productive function, too, in the first period of the defense and war effort. In a great number of lines, wage rates increased more than prices of consumers' goods, so that an effective incentive for taking up work was created. In this respect, also, it seems that the incentive from rising wages can no longer be the main force in mobilizing the labor reserve. As long as the whole supply of civilian goods increased, an increase in real wages was still possible and indeed occurred on a large scale. With the present reduction in civilian supplies, however, an increase in the spendable income of those just induced to take jobs must be offset by a reduction in consumption of those regularly employed. Thus, the use of higher wage rates to induce entry into the labor force must be strictly limited to substandard or inequitable rates. Appeal to patriotism, the pressure resulting from heavy taxes and forced savings rather than the incentive of steadily increasing wages, must be relied upon to increase the active labor force.

From the point of view of postwar reconstruction it probably would have been more desirable to stabilize prices and wages as of, say, spring 1941. Stabilization at that time, however, would have hurt the defense effort. It would have prevented the fullest possible use of labor and facilities during the initial period of the defense program. Price control of a selected number of scarce but essential commodities served as an adequate secondary policy during that period. Now, price stabilization is the appropriate basic policy, as a general price rise with its spiraling effect no longer serves a productive function. In cases in which the present price impedes a production otherwise possible and desirable, an adjustment should be made, either by permitting a carefully limited price or wage increase, or by paying a subsidy in certain cases. The subsidy is preferable in the case of services (like freight) that substantially affect the cost structure of many industries or in the case of life necessities (basic food) in order to prevent such a rise in the cost of living as would induce, in turn, demands for higher wages.

Thus, it appears that in the case of price stabilization there is no real conflict between war and postwar objectives. A general price rise is no longer in the interest of the most intensive war effort, while price stabilization definitely is in the interest of postwar reconstruction. Price stabilization, along with all the implementing policies, contributes to organization of war effort by eliminating the futile race between prices and wages. It contributes to morale by reducing the injustice imposed by an accelerated price rise upon those in a weak economic position, those who do not profit from rising prices and cannot adjust their income to the rising cost of living.—*Gerhard Colm, Economist and Taxation Expert, Adviser to the United States Bureau of the Budget, and Gerald M. Alter. Fortune. O.* '42. *p.* 123.

Wage costs have only recently become a major inflationary force. Unit labor costs did not rise in the first half of the period since August 1939. The substantial rise in the latter half has largely been absorbed out of profits; it has reached the price level in relatively few instances. On the demand side, however, the magnitudes speak for themselves. Wage income to May 1942 increased 79 per cent. While real hourly earnings for all nonagricultural establishments were practically unchanged from

August 1931 to May 1942 there are sharp differences among the various industries. Manufacturing payrolls increased 130 per cent; employment rose 38 per cent, hours lengthened 12 per cent, cash hourly earnings rose 31 per cent, and cash weekly earnings 53 per cent.

In general, the increase in wage rates appears to have accounted for roughly one-fourth of the additional wage income. It is perfectly clear that stabilization of basic wage rates will reduce the acceleration but not stop the rise in wage income. There is, however, a limit to the longer hours and shifts to higher grade employment but no similar limit to rising wage rates.

By holding the lid on prices, the O.P.A. undoubtedly held down wages. But there were two serious limitations upon the indirect control of wages through the control of prices. First, a large and rapidly expanding sector of the economy was producing war materials over which the O.P.A. exercised little or no control. Second, profits were sufficiently fat in some sectors to permit wage increases without price adjustments. And these, in turn, would require a balancing wage increase in other areas where the adjustment could not be made out of profits.

The President's message to Congress on April 27 had called for the general maintenance of wage scales with (1) adjustments for inequalities and (2) elimination of "substandards of living." Nation-wide "stabilization" agreements which initially raised rates were subsequently negotiated in the shipbuilding and construction industries. The War Labor Board's most important decision was the Little Steel Case which provided that workers whose wage rates had increased less than the 13 per cent rise in the cost of living from January 1941 to May 1942 were entitled to have their "peacetime standards reestablished as a stabilization factor."

It was these facts which led the O.P.A. to take the toughest attitude in Washington toward wages. Perhaps the most disturbing fact was the continued adherence to the collective bargaining principle in the face of general administrative determination of prices. The same forces which require wartime control over prices also require the administrative determination of wages. If management and labor are permitted to bargain over the distribution of the product, the government very shortly finds itself paying the bill. In addition, the entire system of war controls is endangered. War profits are abnormal; they should not be industry's to bargain away, nor labor's to demand. In order to function appropriately collective bargaining must operate under more normal conditions.—*Don D. Humphrey, Chief of the Price Analysis and Review Branch, Research Division, O.P.A. American Economic Review. D. '42. p.* 755-6.

Another hole in that dam—and just as serious—involves the matter of wages. Wage increases are also threatening our price ceilings because they are costs and their continued rise inevitably pushes prices higher. But, we must not forget that wages cannot be stabilized if the cost of the food the wage earner must buy also continues upward.

Wage increases, when not accompanied by a corresponding increase in production, are inflationary for two principal reasons. First, they increase labor costs, and thus cause pressure against price ceilings. During the early stages of the war effort, higher wages could be absorbed because of the higher levels of production which reduced unit cost. That happy situation is no longer present in most American industries. From January 1, 1941 to May 1942, unit labor costs increased by an average of 1.1 per cent per month. In the months to come, I look for unit labor costs to rise further—quite apart from any increase in wages rates—what with the loss of younger and skilled workers, introduction of less skilled labor, and inevitable transportation and other delays.

Labor costs in the distribution industries are bound to rise also, because of lower volume, inexperienced workers, and greater burdens of doing business in wartime. Any wage increases in the retail and wholesale trades which must be reflected in prices will find their way directly into a higher cost of living.

The second main effect of higher wages on inflation arises from the pressure of more purchasing power—coming at a time when the volume of consumer foods and services is in a tailspin, as it must be if we are to win this war. The simplest expression of inflation, which all who run should read, is that it occurs when dollars get plentiful and goods get scarcer. We are in that stage right now. The spectacle to marvel at is not that prices and the cost of living are going up—it is spectacular that the overwhelming flood of dollars has not burst the dam wide open.

I do not know where the price level would be if the American people were not paying off their debts at the rate of $4,000,-000,000 a year. Income payments in August were running at the rate of $115,000,000,000 annually. And we used to talk about getting to be a hundred-billion-dollar country. . . .

Wages and salaries alone are now at an annual rate of $76,000,000,000.

Income payments look as if they will increase at the rate of $1,500,000,000 a month. The supply of consumer goods and services will decline about a billion a month. The measure of the inflation problem is thus increasing at the rate of $2,500,-000,000 a month.

All of this means that without prompt and what seems previously to have been considered too drastic action, the people of this country face an extremely critical situation. Conditions would develop which would empty the American family pocket-book of real money. We have passed beyond the point in this war when the interests of special groups with special interests can prevail over the whole people and the common welfare. It is therefore obvious that we must quickly make certain that uncontrolled prices are brought under strict control and that this is done for all products at all levels of distribution.—*Leon Henderson, former Administrator of Office of Price Administration. U.S. Senate. Committee on Banking and Currency. Stabilizing the Cost of Living; Hearings on S.J.Res.*161. '42. *p.* 15-16.

WAGE FREEZING UNCALLED FOR

CEILINGS ON WAGES? [1]

America's greatest internal enemy today is inflation. The battle to defend democracy cannot be won if the nation's economic system is thrown into chaos by runaway prices. Because of the sudden industrial upheaval caused by the shift from production for peacetime needs to production for national defense, chaotic inflation is now a direct threat. Living costs have jumped almost 10 per cent within a year and, unless something is done to control the upward spiral, another 10 per cent boost in prices is likely by next spring.

The American Federation of Labor is determined to do everything within its power not to let this calamity occur. Every jump in prices is a blow to the pocketbook of American workers and their families. It is likewise a blow to industry. Labor will not sit idly by while the American standard of living is being undermined.

In considering this problem and in formulating a constructive policy to prevent inflation, the American Federation of Labor is not moved by selfish motives, but by a patriotic resolution to find the best way out for the entire nation.

We favor the adoption of federal legislation to control prices. We believe that this legislation should remain in force only for the duration of the emergency. We feel that it should apply solely to the prices of commodities and rents. Wages—and profits as well—should be specifically excluded from the measure.

The real need is for a ceiling on basic products and materials which are essential to the well-being of the American people and to the promotion of the national-defense program. Legislation should be designed to prevent the prices of these products and

[1] By William Green, President, American Federation of Labor. *Rotarian.* 60:17, 55-6. January, 1942.

materials from getting out of line. It is unnecessary to freeze all prices since many commodities are so abundant that normal prices are assured.

Certainly there is no justification for the imposition of ceilings on wages. This would be a contradiction of the principles of American democracy and a violation of practical commonsense.

It has long been written into the law of the land that "the labor of a human being is not a commodity or article of commerce." To treat the labor of human beings on a par with commodities is an insult to the aspirations of all Americans. If the American workingman is to be deprived of the opportunity to improve his material welfare, he may well wonder whether the methods and practices of totalitarian states are not being aped in his own land.

In periods of incipient inflation, it is a matter of economic history that wages seldom keep up with prices. The pay envelope always lags behind. It is so now. Although there have been a great many wage increases among workers in American industry during the past year, these pay rises have not kept pace with the upward spiral of prices for the necessities of life. Hence, even though commodity prices are controlled by legislation, wages have a long way to go before catching up with living costs.

When President Roosevelt stated that one-third of the nation is ill fed, ill clothed, and ill housed, he stated a truth borne out by statistics. These figures have not changed materially in the past few years despite many forward strides. Conditions exist among workers in many parts of the country which are a disgrace to America. Millions of American children are being reared under handicaps which are a repudiation of the nation's boast of free opportunity for all. To place a ceiling on wages would mean preventing millions of underprivileged Americans from escaping bitter poverty for themselves and their children.

It is argued by those who favor freezing wages that prices will be forced upward as long as wages are permitted to rise. They claim that every pay increase must and should result in a price increase. Otherwise, they say, the employer must suffer or be squeezed out of business.

Fortunately, that is not in accordance with economic facts. Let us examine the relation of wage increases to price increases in four representative industries this year. In cotton goods a 14 per cent wage increase took place. It added only 5.5 per cent to manufacturing costs, but cotton-goods prices rose 40 per cent. In automobiles a 13 per cent wage increase added only 2.4 per cent to costs and was more than covered by a 5 per cent price increase. In lumber and petroleum there were wage increases of 11 and 6 per cent. These added little or nothing to costs, but prices in each of these industries rose more than 20 per cent.

What is the significance behind this evidence? First, we must realize that wages form only a small part of a company's total expense. Because of this, even a substantial wage increase adds relatively little to total cost of production. The four industries cited above are typical, but the entire picture even more effectively proves this point. In manufacturing as a whole, wage increases added only 2 per cent to total costs this year, but prices rose more than 13 per cent.

Another important factor must be considered. That is the productivity of labor. Industrial research shows that workers today produce much more individually than in years gone by. This is due to improved methods of manufacture and to time-saving inventions. This increase in the productivity of workers averages more than 3 per cent a year. Expanding production and resultant savings in overhead also reduce the unit cost of production. Surely the workingman is entitled to share in the benefits as his labor produces more!

It is not the belated wage increases obtained by American workers that have increased production costs. It is the sky-rocketing prices of materials and commodities. And it is equally true that the increases in production costs have not justified the huge increases in the selling price of the finished product.

Then we encounter another argument. Fear is expressed that if wages continue to increase, the added purchasing power of American workers will itself bring about inflation. It seems to me that these fears are illusionary. Every worker in the United States in the next few years will have to shoulder a heavy burden of taxes to help the government finance the defense program.

And make no mistake about it: the workers are the ones who pay the taxes. Just as profits are controlled by tax legislation, so the added income of America's wage earners will find its way into the coffers of the United States Treasury through new tax levies.

Another control over inflationary spending by workers is the government's defense savings bond drive. Members of the American Federation of Labor are responding to this drive in a wholehearted measure and are investing their savings in these bonds instead of invading the luxury market. Talk of another "silk-shirt era" is a deliberate attempt to create imaginary fears.

I would like to say a word in reply to certain spokesmen for farm groups who appear to favor the freezing of wages. In my opinion, they have adopted a short-sighted attitude. The farmers are prospering today because their normally surplus production is being bought up by the government for shipment to the nations we are aiding in their war on totalitarianism. Once the emergency is over, and these nations regain a self-sustaining basis, this market threatens to disappear.

It is in the interests of the farmers to develop the widest possible domestic market for farm products. The only effective way of accomplishing this is by the wider distribution of the nation's income through the medium of wage increases. When every American workingman earns enough to purchase for himself and his family sufficient proper food, the farmers of America will have the market that they need, the best market in the world right at their front door.

There is no justification for wage freezing, but there is a great need for wage stabilization in America in the interests of labor and industry alike. This stabilization can only be attained through the processes of collective bargaining and the negotiation of fair contracts between employers and trade unions representing their workers. Under such contracts wages can be brought into line with living costs and stabilized for periods of a year or longer. It is the policy of trade unions affiliated with the American Federation of Labor to demand wage increases only when the cost of living, the productivity of the workers, and the profits of the employer justify higher pay.

American Federation of Labor members are not out to ruin employers, because that way they lose their jobs. They want to work in harmony and cooperation with American businessmen. They want to work in close accord with their government in the critical times ahead. In that spirit they offer a practical program of wage stabilization through collective bargaining in place of un-American and unworkable proposals for freezing wages.

LABOR'S VIEW OF WAGE POLICIES FROM NOW ON [2]

Labor's view of wage policies from now on issues from a single point—the winning of the war. The war will be won by the full use of our productive resources. It will require a vigorous, healthy people, inspired by a high morale. It will call upon each of us to make necessary sacrifices.

The primary aim of organized labor's wage policy in this period is to establish for American working people those wages necessary to maintain our workers at the higest possible level of health, efficiency and morale. We believe that the best means of accelerating the production effort is to establish the kind of wages and working conditions that are conducive to maximum output. Most American workers and their families are still living at levels of income wholly insufficient to keep up their health, efficiency and morale. No man or woman can work when he or his family is undernourished. No workers can give his best without adequate medical attention, without decent housing, without a fair share of the necessaries of life.

It is our best judgment, therefore, that within the limitations of our national economy every worker and his family, especially those engaged on war work, must have a real income sufficient to maintain the standards we all accept as adequate.

It is suggested in some quarters, that by seeking to establish adequate wage standards labor fails to make its share of sacrifice. If sacrifices on the part of labor mean the breakdown of the health and efficiency of American workers, then it is true that

[2] By James B. Carey, Secretary, Congress of Industrial Organizations. From "Winning the War." *Academy of Political Science* (New York). *Proceedings*. 20, no. 1. 79-86. May, 1942.

organized labor opposes this kind of deprivation. We believe, however, that labor's sacrifices are being made in the workshop working long hours, coping with the rising accident toll, speeding up output.

The question of wartime wage policies cannot be separated from the other primary factors involved in the war effort. It is an economic and social question with material content and psychological values. Thus, for example, when corporation profit returns for 1941 show a 30 per cent increase over 1940, it is hard for a worker to understand why his wages should be frozen. And those who raise the cry for elimination of the 40-hour week either do not know or else are wilfully blind to its consequences—a wage cut for workers now working more than 40 hours a week. At any rate, it should be evident that the 40-hour week is not a limitation on production, but only a component of the wage structure of many war industries.

But I do not propose to discuss here the distorted issues of a sound wage policy. I propose rather to set forth some of the major principles upon which our views on this subject are founded. First, and most important, I want to say that we are opposed to any scheme of wage freezing or fixing by legislative or other decree. In the words of Senator Brown of Michigan, who handled the Price Control Bill on the floor, and I quote, "Wage adjustments in this country, as in Great Britain, should continue to be made through the normal processes of collective bargaining, assisted by the mediatory activities of the War Labor Board shortly to be established."

The British government has taken the same view in its official white paper on *Price Stabilization and Industrial Policy*, issued on July 22, 1941. It said:

> It is the traditional and well tried practice of the principal industries to regulate wages through their joint voluntary machinery for wage negotiation. Since the outbreak of war, the existing joint voluntary machinery for wage negotiations has operated successfully. Increases in wage rates have been reasonable; the authority of the unions in day-to-day adjustment of wages and conditions has been maintained; the freedom of opportunity to make claims and to have them discussed has enabled industrial peace to be maintained.

The policy of the government, therefore, is to avoid modification of the machinery for wage negotiations and to continue to leave the various voluntary organizations and wage tribunals free to reach their decisions in accordance with their estimate of the relevant facts.

We insist upon this basic principle of the adjusting of wages through collective bargaining because it preserves necessary flexibility and essential freedom. It is responsive to the economic factors of production, and it will not interfere with war production.

I emphasize this last point to remind you once again that labor has surrendered for the duration its right to interrupt production to win bargaining agreements. Labor has kept its pledge. Strikes today are insignificant and they will be more so. At the recent C.I.O. Legislative Conference in Washington, attended by 500 delegates from every branch of the C.I.O., we reiterated that pledge and swore to fulfill it. Wage freezing by edict is unnecessary. It is arbitrary and regimenting. The institutions of collective bargaining represent a confident exercise by management and labor of the faculty to meet and settle their problems. No decree or administrative agency, or statement of policy could be substituted for the multiple arrangements in mines, mills and factories throughout the nation under which collective bargaining committees of management and labor have been established. These arrangements and these committees operate under the final authority of the representatives of the War Labor Board.

It is a sound procedure. It has worked in Great Britain. We have every reason to believe it can work here.

The argument for wage freezing by decree or declaration of policy is not only directed against the procedures of collective bargaining, but it also aims at the establishment of a substantive wage policy. This policy is one of wage freezing. Labor is opposed to wage freezing. We view the issues in the following way:

First. At the present time corporations are able to pay substantial wage increases. The record of business earnings in 1941 and so far in 1942 is ample proof of that fact. Despite increasing taxes, the earnings of enterprises in war production have increased substantially. Let us not be deceived by public reports which may show lower earnings after taxes. These reports often conceal tremendous profits in hidden and unnecessary reserves. Thus, for example, while Bethlehem Steel Corporation reported only 34½ million dollars in net profits after taxes for 1941, an analysis of its financial statement shows that an additional 29 million dollars is kept in so-called special reserves and emergency funds.

Second. In addition to industry's ability to pay wage increases out of its profits, it can provide wage increases without any increase in costs. In other words, substantial wage increases will not require price increases. We rest our position in this regard upon two factors: increased productivity per man-hour and lower cost per unit of production with full production. In the steel industry, for example, during the last eight years labor cost per ton of steel declined 21.9 per cent, although average hourly wages rose 68 per cent in the same period. Like many other industries, steel was geared to profitable operations at 50 per cent of capacity operations. Its price structure is based upon scarcity production. But now with operations over 95 per cent and frequently at 100 per cent of capacity, industry can easily share the benefits of increased productivity and full production with its workers. It is a fair and equitable thing for it to do.

Third. In addition to the ability of industry to pay wage increases and to support the cost without increasing prices, there is the factor that wage increases will be required to prevent a decline in the vigor and morale of our labor forces in the battle of production. The best figures on a minimum, decent standard of living were made a few years ago by the Heller Committee. These figures adjusted to present-day prices call for an annual income of $2,500 for a family of five. The fact is that 70 per cent of American families receive less than $2,000 a year and 34 per cent less than $1,000. We start then with a standard of living for wage-earners which is less than enough to provide healthy vigorous workers. In addition, since the recent wage increases were granted in the spring and summer of 1941, the cost of living has substantially increased and eaten up these money increases.

The Bureau of Labor Statistics shows a 13 per cent increase in the cost of living since March 1941. But this figure is only a very general index. More accurate analysis shows a greater rise in the cost of living to wage-earners on the following basis: Sixty-five per cent of the wage-earners' incomes goes into food, clothing and shelter, and these items have increased, not 13 per cent, but 25 per cent, and as high as 50 per cent in the case of staple foods like potatoes and eggs and rents in congested war production centers. Medical care of the American people is utterly inadequate. The alarming percentage of draft rejections is proof of this. The loss in production due to illness has been estimated at ten days per worker, per year, and this loss lays a terrific toll on our production. At present costs, it would take $400 a year adequately to provide dental and medical care in wage-earners' families, but now they can spend only $75 a year.

We have, moreover, to take into account the increasing taxes burdened upon low income groups. This burden, according to the Temporary National Economical Committee study, has always been high. With the 1941 revenue bill and the tax proposal for 1942, it will be more. We must remember, too, that many American families are still burdened with debts from past years of unemployment. It is argued that price controls will protect the worker against any further increases in the cost of living. In fact, however, it is conceded that costs of living will go up at least a further 10 per cent before price controls become effective. These factors then sum up to the necessity for improvement in wages in order to prevent a serious decline in the health and morale of the working forces of our nation. Together with the ability of industry to pay wage increases without increasing costs and prices, we have laid the foundation for a sound wage policy geared to the needs of the nation.

We then come to the question which has been most seriously advanced against a policy of wage increases. This argument is that diversion to war production reduces the amount of consumer goods. This will mean that there will be an excess of consumer income and the result will be a dangerous inflationary condition. No group in the population has more to fear from inflation, no group suffers more severely than organized labor.

We have considered this problem most carefully, and I submit to you these views.

First. We are opposed to wage freezing and to flat reductions in mass purchasing power as a method of reducing the demand for consumer goods because it is a retrogressive and arbitrary method. It means that the well-to-do groups will give up comforts and luxuries, but wage-earners must give up the necessities of life: food, clothing, housing and medical care. This will seriously impair the war effort which requires vital energies for production.

Second. A flat reduction in mass purchasing power misses the point of our economic situation. The strain on our economy comes from shortages. But these shortages are in specific goods, and in specific means of transportation. We do not have enough copper, steel, tin, pig iron, magnesium, nickel, aluminum and other metals. We do not have enough wool, silks, rubber, burlap, and some drugs and chemicals. We have cut off the production of many consumer goods. There will be no more refrigerators, radios, phonographs, automobiles and washing machines. But with few exceptions such as tea and sugar, we have ample food. Our granaries are bursting. We have cotton, wheat and other cereals. The ordinary household may face a shortage of fuels such as coal and oil due to transportation, but other services are more than ample. Telephones, water, laundry, matches, clothes pins, wooden articles of all kinds, glass and pottery can be increased. Cotton clothing and shoes can be made to fill all reasonable consumer demands. We can provide medical care, tobacco, books, soaps and toiletries, recreational and educational activities. All these things are things wage-earners buy. The point I wish to emphasize is that we can produce these things without any significant drain upon our war effort. On the contrary, a healthy, vigorous working force is essential to our war effort. Our problem today is not one of limited resources or labor supply, but rather the organization and use of our resources. The production of specific and needed goods is not held up by shortages, but by specific bottlenecks in production. We have overcome business-as-usual in war production to a large degree. We need to do the same job in essential civilian production.

Let me repeat again that families with incomes under $2,500 a year spend 65 per cent of the income for food, clothing and shelter, and the balance can readily be absorbed by taxes, recreation, medical care, savings and education. There can be extra milk for the children, beef instead of pork, and a cigar and a beer for the head of the family, teeth can be filled and tonsils removed. We can have more shoes and more clothing and the services for personal care and cleanliness. We can and we must attend to the well-being of our people without diverting from war production. We can eliminate gadgets and provide the simple elements of a healthy, sane life for our people.

The fact is that a blanket wage decrease reduces mass purchasing power, but it will not reduce the demand for articles that compete for war production.

I do not wish to be misunderstood—labor is prepared to make all necessary sacrifices willingly, but it is not willing to permit bottlenecks in production that cause unnecessary and severe hardships. We are for full production. We have proposed measures looking toward full production. We are against bottlenecks that prevent the use of skilled laborers existing in minority groups, such as Negroes. We have pointed to the fact that in the New Jersey area only 50 per cent of potential facilities are being utilized, and our report was confirmed by Mr. Nelson. We are urging upon the army the use of a standard engine in tanks of the same type. At present these tanks are being made with different engines by different companies. The result is to cause a hopeless maintenance problem when these tanks are actually in combat. It is also wasteful. We have prepared labels with black borders carrying the legend: "This machine is working for Hitler," and these labels will be placed on every idle machine.

By the same token, we must organize our production for essential civilian needs. Let me cite a clear example. The great Ford bomber plant at Willow Run, thirty miles outside Detroit, is nearing completion. It will require about 100,000 workers, the majority of them with families. Housing for these workers is as important to the production of the bombers as is aluminum. We have undertaken to plan full production of aluminum. We have not done so for housing. Yet we have potential building materials, using substitutes for metals, to do the job. But it will be done only by planning, from the timber forests and glass factories to the point of fabrication and erection. And a sound wage policy with common sense organization will provide workers with good homes, good diets and adequate clothing so that they can produce bombers and yet more bombers.

Our views on wage policies from now on are, therefore, based upon a consideration of the total factors for production in the winning of this war. We insist that the procedure for the determination of wages should be made through the institution of collective bargaining under the War Labor Board, with a guarantee against any interruption of production for any cause. We are opposed to wage freezing because we think it is economically unsound and socially unjust, and it impairs the vitality and morale of our production forces. We rest our views upon an appraisal of the production forces of our nation. We submit that upon these factors, wage policies can be determined through collective bargaining that will provide justified wages and necessary increases to take up essential goods.

A wage policy of this kind must be coördinated with effective price controls, equitable rationing of scare articles, and full use of our productive resources.

It will have a single objective, to win the war.

A. F. OF L.'S ANTI-INFLATION PROGRAM [3]

In the summer of 1942 it became clear that price control alone cannot avert inflation. The Price Control Administration was slow and deficient, key farm prices were exempt from control, and fiscal controls necessary to stabilize our economy were lacking. No decisive measures were taken to control costs on war contracts, and Congress persistently shirked its responsibility to curb excessive corporate and individual

[3] *American Federation of Labor. Report of Proceedings,* 1942. p. 217-18. The Federation. Washington, D.C. 1942.

profits. To cover up these deficiencies in price administration a smoke-screen of propaganda was raised over the country in an attempt to force freezing of wages. By July, 1942, the campaign to freeze wages reached overwhelming proportions. On July 20, President Green transmitted to the President of the United States a declaration on wages and inflation which contained a broad program of inflation control. This declaration stated:

> Every American working for wages is personally and vitally concerned in the nation's effort to avert inflation. Every wage earner is equally concerned in the nation's wage policy and the effect of this policy on the workers' contribution to maximum war production.
>
> Every American worker will do his very utmost to help his country win. But he will insist that our common sacrifice be equal, fair and just. To assure equality, fairness and justice to all in the war effort, the American Federation of Labor offers the following program of inflation control:
>
> 1. Wage adjustment through the process of collective bargaining between labor and management. All disputed wage issues, except those covered by wage stabilization agreements, shall be settled by (a) direct negotiation, (b) conciliation and arbitration, and (c) submission to the National War Labor Board for final decision.
>
> 2. Voluntary wage stabilization agreements are now in effective operation in the shipbuilding and construction industries, covering more than 2,500,000 workers. Voluntary wage stabilization agreements shall be negotiated and executed in other key industries and occupations with wage stabilization boards established in each, similar to the boards now in operation.
>
> 3. A Wage Policy Commission shall be established consisting of an equal number of representatives of labor, management and the government, to coordinate and unify wage policies and to prescribe such agreed policies to all government agencies whose activities are related to wage adjustment directly or indirectly.
>
> 4. Payment of wage increases in war bonds, cashable after the war. Future wage increases for the same work shall be paid in whole or in part in a special series of war bonds not convertible into cash until after the war, except in distress situations. The use of such bonds will prevent dislocation of our wage structure and will enable workers to build up a reserve of buying power to be released after the war to sustain our economy and prevent unemployment when the armed forces and war industries are demobilized.
>
> 5. Immediate application of effective control of excessive corporate profits through taxation and through integrated cost control on all government purchasing.

6. A program of progressive income taxation designed to prevent personal profiteering in wartime, and increased contributions for an expanded social security program with wider coverage which would give the mass of our wage earners a measure of economic security when war employment ends.

7. Voluntary contribution by all citizens to the cost of winning the war by largest possible investment of their earnings in war bonds.

8. Effective control of prices on consumer goods at the retail, wholesale, and manufacturing levels, and control of rents.

9. Rationing of all scarce commodities to distribute them fairly among all and to prevent profiteering and hoarding.

10. Price ceilings on materials and equipment produced on government account cannot and will not keep down the cost nor eliminate profiteering in war production. Price ceilings on war contracts tend to retard war output. They are inflexible, unrealistic and cumbersome to administer. In expanded production unit costs are constantly reduced and military specifications are constantly changing. Maximum economy in government spending for war goods, combined with maximum output and maximum speed, can only be achieved through unified cost control. We recommend that the necessary technical service be established in the Executive Office of the President to direct and unify cost control in all procurement and war production agencies.

On April 27 the President of the United States laid down a seven-point program to control the cost of living. The program called for stabilization of profits; stabilization of wages; and stabilization of farm prices. It also provided for ceilings on prices of consumer goods and rents; purchase of war bonds; rationing; and credit curtailment. The President told the nation that the cost of living can be stabilized only if profits, wages and farm prices are stabilized at the same time. He said "The important thing to remember is that each one of these points is dependent on the others if the whole program is to work." This he laid down as the essential principle of equality of sacrifice, of equality of privilege for all to work for victory of democracy by democratic means.

To date this principle has been disregarded. Only wages are being subjected to control. Exorbitant personal and corporate profits from war production are daily reported in the press. Even greater profits are concealed by clever accounting devices. Food prices continue to rise. There are no price ceilings on some 25 farm commodities.

Labor must not be made the scapegoat for the administrative deficiency in the inflation control to date. There must be one unified policy of inflation control equally applied to all groups and enforced by active and free participation, willing and understanding, on the part of the people themselves.

Labor will accept wage stabilization which is accompanied by stabilization of profits and other income payments. Labor insists that wage stabilization be achieved not by arbitrary decree but by agreement. Wage stabilization must not preclude correction of substandard rates, elimination of inequalities, nor adjustment of rates to compensate for increased skill and output.

The American Federation of Labor proposes the above program as a constructive and workable plan of inflation control under which democratic procedures will be safeguarded, collective bargaining will continue to be the major instrumentality of wage stabilization and cost of living will become firmly anchored.

Labor can and should be a responsible partner in winning the war. The adoption of our plan will enable American workers to increase speed and productivity of war industry as free and willing citizens striving mightily for victory of democracy over dictatorship and enslavement.

On September 7, 1942, the President addressed another message to Congress in which he reiterated the principles of his April 27 program and asked for the enactment of legislation by October 1 which would provide effective and equitable control of farm prices, as well as adequate tax legislation.

On September 14 a Joint Resolution was introduced in the Senate conferring upon the President broad powers to stabilize prices, wages, salaries "and other factors affecting the cost of living . . . on the basis of the levels which existed on August 15, 1942." The Resolution provided that maximum prices on farm commodities be established at 100 per cent parity. It called for wage stabilization which would permit adjustments contemplated by the Wage and Hour Law and would make possible correction of "gross inequalities." The Resolution precluded reduction of wages or salaries for any particular work below the highest wages or salaries paid for such work between January 1 and September 15, 1942. A conflicting bill was offered in the House by Representative Steagall, Chairman of the Banking and Currency Committee. This bill proposed to peg farm prices at 100 per cent of a new and higher parity, opening a way for a new advance of farm prices over a wide front.

This Joint Resolution reflected the feeling on the part of Congress that action was necessary to prevent the disruption of American economy in the war crisis. The country was clearly suffering from the lack of adequate inflation controls.

It was abundantly clear that the Office of Price Administration's program did not prove effective in protecting the American public from inflationary pressures generated by inadequate wartime economic organization. To an important degree O.P.A.'s failure to meet its responsibility fully was obscured by three basic factors. First, there was a very substantial increase in the savings of wage earners which resulted in a voluntary curtailment of expenditures for consumer goods. Second, the public responded wholeheartedly to the War Savings Bonds campaign, and large purchases of war bonds were made by workers throughout the land. Finally, the American public responded to the demands of the war by its broad acceptance of the rationing programs and its unwillingness to hoard or foster black markets.

The personal discipline on the part of the large majority of the American public was extraordinary and heartening. A large share of the available expendable income was effectively contracted through self-imposed savings activity of the people.

The O.P.A.'s price control program, however, was not couched in the stern terms demanded by the economic requirements of war. The price orders issued prior to the general maximum price regulation largely evaded the problem of turning the trend of industrial prices to lower levels. Instead they were carefully planned to disturb as little as possible the peacetime pricing policies of business. Only too often industries, after striving mightily to bring their wholesale prices up to the O.P.A. ceilings, found prices receding to levels considerably below these ceilings. Many attempts, based on premises as unjustified as they were uncritical, riddle the price ceilings which were set at more realistic levels.

In the field of rationing O.P.A. sought to postpone as long as possible this necessary but unpopular step. The top O.P.A. officials obviously misjudged the deadly earnestness of the American people, willing and eager to make sacrifices provided equality of sacrifice is maintained.

O.P.A. also lacked courage in attacking the price structures of the initial processors of our raw materials—chiefly controlled by giant corporate aggregates. Many of the basic raw material prices ran riot under the pressure of war demands in the last two years. Some of the greatest increases in raw material prices were hidden, taking effect through the elimination of substantial discounts from posted prices or through the refusal to offer lower priced lines for sale.

The American Federation of Labor's proposal for control of costs on war contracts was designed as a practical plan to take profits out of war at the source and in a way which would not impede maximum production, but stimulate it.

The 1941 Revenue Act provided a thoroughly ineffective basis for profit control. The General Motors 1941 income before taxes was $489,743,000, and its profit after taxes was $221,408,-000. Bethlehem Steel's profit after taxes was $50,000,000. Corporations reported profits as high as thirty times their capitalization. There were many instances of enormous salaries paid to corporation executives. The major portion of excess profits was frequently concealed through rigged depreciation accounts, special reserves, and many other accounting devices.

The government relied chiefly on price ceilings and price adjustment boards to control profiteering on war contracts. The Price Adjustment Boards review war contracts and use their influence with companies to scale down the prices paid for the manufacture of war equipment and weapons. An inadvertently published directive to Price Adjustment Boards created a national scandal, spelling out the methods by which the contractors' profit was to be protected under this procedure.

The O.P.A. attempted to apply price ceilings to contract prices on war production items in their final assembly. This device puts a premium on high costs and provides incentive for inefficiency. Price ceilings in rapidly expanding production are ineffective controls. They must, of necessity, be set high enough to blanket in the high-cost producers and invite the efficient low-cost producers to escalate their costs. Economies achieved through lowered per unit cost, made possible by the expanding volume, cannot be determined or recaptured in the absence of industry-wide cost control.

Labor promptly demanded that the O.P.A. keep its hands off the control of munitions prices, so that inefficiences and inflation would not be frozen into the production of war implements and equipment. Instead, Labor proposed to establish a system of integrated cost controls on an industry-wide basis to make it possible to get costs, prices and profits down to equitable levels.

The battle against inflation has been a losing battle also because of the absence of an effective fiscal policy. Installment credit control on consumer's goods was applied by the Federal Reserve Board in 1941 and was tightened in 1942. This curtailment of installment buying was regressive, as it curtailed the buying power of the low income families only, permitting disproportionate spending to those who had cash. Being forced to rely largely on borrowing, the Treasury permitted much borrowing that was as clearly inflationary. In its War Savings Bond issues only half of the Treasury's quota was filled by the sale of the so-called "people's bond," and even those were mostly in denominations from $500 to $1,000. The other half was bought by investors in denominations of from $1,000 to $10,000. It was certain that a substantial portion of bond purchases did not effect curtailment of consumer income, but represented investment of idle cash funds.

Other Treasury borrowings included offerings designed to tap the funds of savings banks, corporations, trust companies, and insurance companies. The great bulk of the Treasury borrowing, however, was from commercial banks—a frankly inflationary device. When the government borrows from a bank, the bank simply sets up deposits for government account until the legal minimum of cash reserve is reached. Bank borrowing by the Treasury creates new money. Most important of all, it places the bulk of the public debt in the hands of the banks and not of the people.

Labor calls for an indivisible program of inflation along the entire economic front. It urges a program which is geared to the maximum war production above everything else. It insists on setting up postwar credits through the special social security tax proposed in the Eliot bill. It firmly believes that it is possible to effect a program which can achieve this without departing from the principles of equality, fairness and justice, without abandoning the procedures of democracy, and without outlawing collective bargaining.

WAGES AND ARGUMENTS [4]

The conflict is not inflation v. armament output, since the men and women who produce the implements of war can be supplied with that level of real wages necessary to maintain their optimum efficiency and good health without adding to the dangers of inflation. This is so for the following reasons:

1. The underlying theory of the inflationary gap is a libel on the American people. In a word, this theory holds that an excess of active consumers' income over available consumers' goods causes competition among the holders of this excess purchasing power that inevitably bids up prices on the relatively scarce goods. I am one who holds a few pennies of this excess buying power and I am not using it to bid up prices. I won't pay an uneconomic value for any piece of goods. I won't pay $90 for a $37.50 radio. Nor will the large majority of my fellow citizens. Look at the facts in the Pittsburgh workshop.

An electrical-appliance store on Wood Street has its windows covered with a sign reading, "We Still Have a Complete Stock of Radios, Washers, Sweepers." There's no rush to grab up these "consumer durables." The daily papers carry ads begging customers to buy "GAS RANGES $10 TO $25 LOWER THAN OUR CEILING PRICES!" No automobiles have come off the assembly lines for weeks, yet the last cars for the duration go begging for buyers. . . .

But on the foodstuffs, the inflationary gapists reply, surely the excess income will bid up prices. The answer to this is not wage-freezing, but democratic rationing of scarce goods and effective price control. In this type of program an effective administrative aid, which is now virtually unused, is the extensive labor-union machinery throughout industrial America.

[4] From article by Harold J. Ruttenberg, United Steel Workers of America. *New Republic*. 107:18-19. July 6, 1942.

Give an ounce of official recognition to the steel local union in Homestead, Pennsylvania, for example, and there will be few, if any, violations of ceiling prices or rationing rules there. The local union leaders and committeemen would see to that.

2. The idea of wage-freezing overlooks the elementary fact that, like any other army, the army of production workers travels on its stomach. You should see a charging-machine operator after he has finished charging a battery of open-hearth furnaces. He has lost from three to five pounds. In a day a blast-furnace worker or a steel rolling-mill heater loses several pounds. These men don't eat salads and drink iced tea for their meals. Their work demands that they eat good wholesome food, and plenty of it. And a 15-per cent wage cut—the extent to which rising living costs have depleted the real income of steel workers since their last wage increase in April, 1941—restricts their ability to get such food and, in turn, impairs their productive efficiency.

Work in steel and other vital material and armament industries is more than physical effort. It is strenuous mentally. Add to the normal incident of mental fatigue the extra hazards of growing, unfilled needs of the family, mounting grocery debts, an increasingly scanty lunch basket, and the average industrial worker not only drops in his productive efficiency but is more likely to suffer injury on the job and greater lost time through sickness and weakened physical strength. The level of industrial wages at the start of the war or at their highest point since September, 1939, has never been adequate to provide living standards of good health, efficiency and security. In steel the annual wage is $500 below such a level, and in other industries as much as $1,000 below.

No argument is made that this level can be reached during the war. But certainly the inadequacies of industrial workers' earnings show that they cannot be further depleted now except at the expense of armament output. On April 29 of this year, on behalf of the then Steel Workers' Organizing Committee (now the United Steelworkers of America), I wrote Price Administrator Henderson:

I am enclosing a list of comparative retail food prices for the city of Cincinnati, Ohio, for April, 1941, and April, 1942. This list covers the basic staple food items purchased by workers' families. The percentage increases in prices for these foodstuffs, soaps, etc., range from 14 per cent to 106 per cent, with most of them being in excess of 35 per cent. The situation in Cincinnati is typical of industrial cities and towns throughout the country.

The last general increase in wages in the steel industry took place on April 1, 1941, and almost a year has elapsed since there has been a general wage increase in any major basic armament or war-production industry.

Your order of yesterday freezing prices for these essential foodstuffs at the highest level for the month of March, 1942, is a gross inequity, works an undue hardship upon the industrial workers of America and is an injustice of such a magnitude that it cannot be compared with any previous act of the federal government in the course of the war.

In view of this gross injustice, the Office of Price Administration should either stabilize retail prices at the levels of April 1, 1941, or should petition the National War Labor Board to stabilize real wages at that level. . . .

This letter drew no reply. Unless the efforts of America's production workers to stabilize their real wages at that level essential for maximum war output draw better results, there will be cause for rejoicing in Berlin and Tokyo.

3. Another fallacy of freezing the money incomes of industrial workers is that it concentrates the government's debt in the hands of the upper-income groups. Industrial workers are suffering not only from cost-of-living wage cuts, but from the loss of supplementary incomes of sons in the armed services. This loss has not begun to be made up by daughters going into war work, nor will it ever be substantially. The differentials between the earnings of workers at the bottom and top of the scale mean that for some workers a wage adjustment will more than enable them to buy the necessities necessary to achieve full production. This extra income, and even some income that could better be spent for necessities from the viewpoint of armament output, will be drained off into heavier war-bond purchases.

This is essential for an additional reason than that the money is needed to finance the war. From every sound social and economic consideration the government debt incurred during the war should be distributed equitably among all income groups. Without at least a wage adjustment to offset much of the rising-living-cost losses, industrial workers, who constitute the bulk of the low-income groups, will be unable to acquire their proper proportion of the federal government's war debt. The secretary of a steelworkers' local union, Melville Kress, U.S.A. Local 1416, Pittsburgh Screw and Bolt Corporation, writes me:

> I enclose a copy of a telegram sent to the president of the Pittsburgh Screw and Bolt Corporation by Henry Morgenthau Jr., concerning purchases of government bonds. We made two canvasses, and to date the best we have been able to accomplish in the sale of bonds is about 3 per cent of the gross payroll. Of course, if the anticipated wage adjustment of one dollar per day ever becomes real, there is no question in my mind that our local will subscribe to the objective 10 per cent gross payroll (or better) purchases suggested by Mr. Morgenthau.

This situation is not unusual. Forced bond sales or compulsory savings are not the answer, since they would only further impair the workers' ability to maintain their optimum productive efficiency. A substantial wage adjustment, like the dollar a day sought by the steelworkers, is the answer most consistent with the maximum output of armaments.

4. Wage-freezing is the suspension of collective bargaining. Not all the emasculating amendments to the National Labor Relations Act of the Smiths and Coxes could do as much damage to the cause of industrial democracy as the arbitrary stoppage of wage adjustments through the regular processes of collective bargaining. A prime objective of collective bargaining is the redistribution of the proceeds of production. The mounting profits of war industries emphasize the necessity for not impairing the strength of unions to achieve this objective. The purpose now is not, as in peacetime, to redistribute the income of industry to raise the living standards of workers, but to enable workers to provide themselves and their families with (1) the essentials necessary for maximum production and (2) a few additional dollars to purchase their share of war bonds.

As a matter of fact, to freeze wages now would further aggravate the inequitable distribution of the national income, since payrolls are only rising at the rate of 11 per cent over last year while the national income is rising at the rate of 21 per cent. Thus to freeze wages during the war is to throw a still greater proportion of the national income into the hands of the upper-income groups. Labor should at least be able to maintain its peacetime proportionate share of the national income during the war.

The morale of human beings cannot be based exclusively on exhortations to sacrifice and produce. I do not disparage these, but more is needed. Any sound basis for improving morale should have substance, and wage-freezing will undermine morale more effectively and quickly than any other single national policy that might be pursued. It is not only unsound national policy for this reason, but it would discourage union membership and accordingly weaken the ability of the labor movement to make its greatest contribution to winning the war. Wage-freezing would (1) virtually destroy incentives to raise production and (2) kill the growing effectiveness of joint union-management committees to step up production.

That the destruction of labor unions, and not the winning of the war, is the real objective of many proponents of wage-freezing makes this entire concept all the more destructive of the true purposes of democracy.

INFLATION AND LOW INCOME GROUPS [5]

It may be argued, the low income groups buy some goods as to which shortages exist. Their incomes exert some inflationary pressure. Taxation or wage ceilings, though concededly hard on low income groups, are needed to reduce that inflationary pressure.

I think it is clear that some measures are needed to deal with such shortages. But not a reduction in low incomes

[5] From article by Jerome R. Hellerstein, Tax Counsel to the Trustees of Associated Gas and Electric Corporation, New York. *Taxes*. 21:110-11. February, 1943.

through taxation, compulsory savings or wage ceilings. The trouble with such measures is that they are too crude, for they cut down on *total* incomes. They cut down on the low income recipient's ability to buy the goods which are plentiful, as well as the goods which are scarce. The taxpayer may, for example, be prevented from buying milk for his children or from going to the beauty parlor, or he may have to cut down on the movies as a result of his tax bill. Yet, we may have enough milk and beauty parlors and too many movie houses. To cut down willy-nilly on low incomes because there are shortages in some goods bought by such income groups just doesn't make sense. It would constitute a grave threat to the health and morale of the American people who are fighting this war in the factories, the shops and the homes.

Measures designed to cut down all incomes, including low incomes, in order to relieve the pressure in the market place on scarce goods are also objectionable because they are highly undemocratic. They represent a form of rationing of available supplies in which a well-filled pocketbook is the ration card. People with comfortable and large incomes will still be able to buy whatever is in the shops despite sales taxes, gross income taxes, lowered exemptions and higher rates, but the low income groups will have to cut down on their needs. Such a policy does not fit in with the pattern of a democracy fighting a people's war.

How then shall we deal with inflation? The proper role of taxation is to siphon off the incomes which present the greatest inflationary menace—principally through stiff income taxes on the brackets above $2,000 a year and through the reduction in such incomes by means of heavy corporate taxes. Not only will such taxes hit the mass purchasing power, but quite as important, they will not undermine the health, efficiency or morale of the soldiers of production on the home front.

Such taxation will, of course, by no means do the whole job. We need a whole "portfolio of measures" to safeguard our economy against runaway inflation.

We need the price control, rent control, salary and wage stabilization, credit control and bond purchases which are integral parts of the President's seven point anti-inflation program.

We need the full employment of all our productive resources—and that means small plants as well as large.

We need the conversion of every available plant to the maximum production of the most vital war and civilian goods—without hindrance by personal considerations as to postwar positions or profits.

We need to end the hoarding of inventories of precious metals and machines and to utilize these resources in the national interest.

We need to stop the colossal waste of manpower resulting from discrimination against race, color, creed and nationality, from unemployment and from inadequate training.

We need to curtail the use of men and machines in such fields as advertising, which now serve largely to promote inflation.

We need all-out rationing of all goods and services where shortages exist or threaten, so as to distribute the burden of sacrifice with some measure of equality.

Many of these measures are settled, national policy, but few are being carried out effectively. The wage stabilization program has probably been carried out more completely and more effectively than any other plank in the President's anti-inflation program, through the work of the National War Labor Board.

If I am right in my conclusion as to the role of taxation in curbing inflation, Congress completely missed the mark in a big way by its emphasis in the Revenue Act of 1942 on low incomes. The crushing new burdens imposed on low income groups through the 5 per cent gross income tax on incomes in excess of $12 a week, the lowered income tax exemptions and high basic rates cannot be justified under the guise of fighting inflation. What is required is additional heavy taxation on the groups above $2,000 through measures such as the Treasury's proposed spending tax, limited to the higher income groups.

There are other features of the national anti-inflation program which we have adopted but which we are not enforcing. Consider price control and rationing, two of our most important weapons in fighting inflation. Statutes, regulations and orders have been duly adopted and promulgated in Washington. But what has happened in the market place? A black market on tires and gasoline has developed. Violations and evasions of O.P.A.'s general price order are rife. Indeed, as now set up, I do not believe price control and rationing can be adequately enforced. The job is too vast. The problem too complicated and the possibilities of avoidance and evasion too numerous for any American governmental agency to enforce.

The job of enforcement can be done effectively in one way only—by going to the people for help. For example, suppose the O.P.A. were to encourage the formation of tenants' unions in every building or in every neighborhood, what chance would the landlord have to get away with rent rises above ceilings, or to cut down on painting or repairs or services, with an active tenants' union on the job? And suppose the O.P.A. were to help organize consumers into price brigades, with the help of labor unions and consumers organizations? With every consumer a price warden, with a price brigade ready to enforce consumers' rights through complaints, suits for damages under the Price Control Act, picketing and boycotts of the violators—with such measures we would get somewhere in price control. And through educational campaigns conducted by thousands of consumer groups, we would even be able to deal with the most serious price problem of all, "indirect inflation" through the deterioration in the quality of goods.

This is a people's war. Inflation is the people's battle. It will never be won unless the people are called upon to see to it that the battle is won in the shops and in the stores.

There is a profound struggle going on in connection with the drive against inflation. The combatants are divided into two camps. On one side are those who lay primary emphasis on cutting down the purchasing power of low income groups. On the other, are those who advocate effective price and rent control, all-out rationing and heavy taxes on middle and higher income groups.

This struggle between the two basic methods of fighting inflation goes deeper than deciding who is to bear the brunt of sacrifices for war. All-out rationing and price control mean a widely regulated economic system, not controlled by price bidding or monopolies, but by government. Under all-out rationing and price control, the producer will create the goods needed by the nation, with materials provided under government sanction, and the merchant will sell them, not to the highest bidder, but at governmentally controlled prices through the democratic ration book.

The key to the vigorous opposition voiced in some quarters to effective all-out rationing and price control is, I suggest, a deep seated hostility to a controlled economy. Perhaps a controlled war economy will work so well that we will carry over to our peacetime economy a large degree of governmental control of our economic life. The fear of a controlled economy, plus the desire to place the burden of paying for the war on the masses of the people, are important motivations behind the widespread demand for soaking the poor in the guise of staving off inflation.

COMMENTS ON INFLATION [6]

The "gap" theory—and I emphasize that it is a theory—supplies on the level of practical policy the only justification for a large number of reactionary economic policies. It is exactly this theory, and no other, which supplies the pretext for attacks on mass purchasing power as expressed in the provisions of the 1942 Revenue Act, in the coming drive on taxes for 1943, and in many aspects of policy on wages.

Earlier this year, the Treasury stated correctly that the purpose of the war taxes is to raise money to win the war, to pay the cost of the war. But today the Treasury experts are no longer talking about raising money to pay the cost of the war, they are talking instead about cutting purchasing power to combat the "gap." For these backward economic steps no other

[6] From article by Lyle Dowling, Executive Assistant at the National Office of the United Electrical, Radio and Machine Workers of America, C.I.O. *Science and Society,* 7:53-4. Winter, 1943.

explanation has been offered save the erroneous one that mass purchasing power is *per se* "inflationary."

A variation of the "gap" school is the school which holds that mass purchasing power is "just slightly" inflationary; but this is really little different from the "gap" theory itself.

Underlying the "gap" theory is the false notion that because certain goods and services are needed more for the war effort, therefore they should be priced higher. In other words, if a man owns a copper mine and the demand for copper increases, the "gap" theorists hold that the increased demand causes a price rise—but the fact is, of course, that the increased demand has merely amplified the opportunity for profiteering. The fact is that the increased demand, when the nation is waging a war for survival, is no adequate reason whatsoever for a price rise in copper.

A second assumption underlying the "gap" theory is that price ceilings cannot possibly be enforced. I have heard a representative of the Office of Price Administration say that, from the first, half the staff of O.P.A. has been convinced that price ceilings cannot be enforced; and it goes without saying that such a defeatist position by the enforcing agency makes it impossible to get very far nationally in the handling of our economic problems.

There is no such thing as prices going up by themselves. It requires a specific, volitional action to raise a price. Every rise in price on a raw material, power, cost of money level, or on the wholesale level brings in its train hundreds, thousands of price rises at the retail level.

In the last analysis, every price has but two components: the labor cost of the item, and the profits cost, including that special form of profit called ground rent. We can therefore conclude that when, as at the present time, prices are generally rising while the labor cost per unit remains stationary or rises less rapidly than the prices, then somebody must be the richer in profits for such rises. We see, then, that profits are of crucial importance in inflationary rises of prices.

It seems to me that we have to develop two main lines of approach to these economic problems.

For one, there is the campaign to bring about a total approach to the economic problem as one problem—one problem the tax aspects of which, the wage and price aspects of which, the production aspects of which can be solved only altogether, as a single problem. That is what we call the total approach to the problem, and both the C.I.O. and the A.F. of L. convention resolutions embody this realization of the need for a total approach.

But the practical situation which confronts us is that, while the labor unions are urging a total approach, it is the other kind of approach that is in fact being made by the government.

Therefore, while we continue to work for the total approach, the unions find themselves obliged as well to match the reactionary tactics on each separate aspect of the economic problem—the piecemeal handling of taxes, the piecemeal handling of wage policy, etc. We want to have a total approach to taxation as one aspect of the central problem—but so long as the decisions as to the manner of approach are other than those we would desire, so long as the piecemeal approach prevails, we are obliged to handle the problems arising from such a faulty approach.

PRICE CONTROL BILL AND WAGES [7]

1. The O.P.A. and Wage Control

The Price Administrator emphatically opposed the inclusion of any kind of wage control in the Price Control Bill. His view was upheld by votes on the issue in the House Committee on Banking and Currency.

On numerous occasions in his testimony before the House and Senate, Mr. Henderson, Administrator of Price Control, definitely and specifically requested that wage control not be established in connection with price control.

[7] Steel Workers Organizing Committee, National War Labor Board. Brief submitted in the matter of Steel Workers Organizing Committee and Bethlehem Steel Company and others. p. 95-103. 1943.

The House Committee on Banking and Currency had before it several proposals, including bills and amendments by Mr. Gore and Mr. Robertson, which would have placed wage control in the bill. All such proposals were voted down in the committee. The committee's report said:

It (the bill) does not give to the administrator power to establish ceilings on wages or salaries. (p. 4)

When the bill went to the House floor, several amendments for including wage control were presented on the floor. On November 25th, Mr. Williams of Missouri, who conducted a large part of the hearings and represented the committee on the floor of the House on the bill set forth extensively the reasons why the committee did not include wage freezing or wage controls in the bill. He said among other things:

In the first place, no nation in the world has placed price control and wage fixing in the same governmental agency.

In the next place, during all these years Congress has passed labor legislation and we have well established labor policies in this nation. If the opinion, the order, or the decree of a price administrator is substituted for voluntary negotiation and agreement between labor and industry on the question of wages, then all the labor legislation which we have passed is destroyed. The two cannot stand together. Somebody said we can repeal all of our labor legislation. Of course we can. We can do that. There is not any question about our power to do it. But I do not believe there is anybody in this House who would advocate that.

The views expressed by Mr. Williams prevailed and all amendments proposed to establish controls over wages were decisively defeated.

The Senate Committee upheld the view of the House and reported the bill without any wage freezing or controls. The Report of the Senate Committee on Banking and Currency (p. 12), begins its discussion of wages by saying:

The House Bill specifically forbids the administrator from establishing ceilings, or other direct controls, over wages. We concur in this provision and recommend that no such power should be given to the administrator.

The Senate Committe specifically rejected proposals for the placing of wage freezing or wage control in the Price Control

Bill. The Senate approved the committee's position in the matter.

Senator Prentiss Brown in presenting the bill for the Senate Banking and Currency Committee, made a special point of discussing the problem of wage freezing and wage control. He said in part:

> The bill specifically provides that nothing in the act shall be construed to authorize the regulation of compensation paid by an employer to any of his employes. Control of wages in connection with price control is, on the one hand, administratively impossible, and on the other hand undesirable from the point of view of public policy. (Congressional Record, January 7, 1942)

2. Congress Opposes Wage Freezing and Wage Controls

The action of the House Committee in rejecting proposals for wage control was clearly and definitely not only a decision not to institute wage control in connection with price control, but also a decision not to institute wage freezing or wage control at all.

This position was clearly set forth by Mr. Williams speaking on behalf of the committee to the House on November 25, 1941. At that time he said:

> We have heard in recent months that you cannot control prices without controlling and fixing wages.

He characterized this position as a "hoax" and a "canard."

He pointed out in the same statement that the price increases which had already taken place had not been caused by wage increases and that this in particular was made clear by the extensive profit history of industry in the first nine months of 1941. He said:

> When you are dealing with prices, you are dealing with an inanimate object. When you are dealing with wages you are dealing with a living, pulsating human being. Outside of the human element that is involved in it, I want to lay down the general proposition that to fix wages by legislative act or fix wages by the edict or the decree or the decision of a price administrator is doing an absolute injustice to the laboring man of this country. . . .

Fixing wages is not only impractical and impossible of administration, but it is inequitable and an injustice to labor. It is absolutely unenforceable. It is unconstitutional. . . .

If legislation of the kind and character suggested by the gentleman from Tennessee (Mr. Gore) or any other legislation fixing wages and not fixing profits, is enacted by this Congress into law, the wage difficulties which we have had already will be but a gentle breeze and a soft zephyr compared to the cyclonic whirlwind of protest, discord, dissension, strife, and strikes that will envelop us if we substitute the edicts and dictates of a price administrator for the time-honored voluntary bargaining agreements between industry and labor.

The Senate Committee indicated the same point of view, saying in its report (page 12):

The problems of wage control are totally dissimilar from those of price control and are extraordinarily complex. . . .

A broader and more fundamental objection to the regulation of wages by techniques similar to those appropriate for the control of prices lies in the fact that wage control is income control. Price control itself constitutes a limitation upon the total income derived from production, but this must be sharply distinguished from control over the apportionment of that income among those contributing to its production. Under normal circumstances, the competition of the market limits the extent to which prices, wages, salaries, or any other income may rise. Businessmen and labor recognize that prices and wages can be raised only at the expense of sales volume and employment. Wage bargaining proceeds on that basis. Under emergency circumstances the establishment of maximum prices serves precisely the same function. Maximum price regulation, by limiting the total value of output, limits the sum available for apportionment. It sets the framework within which this apportionment may be determined upon bases mutually agreeable to the parties involved.

In other words, even under price control collective bargaining should continue to take place for the division of industrial income between labor and capital.

The committee further said in its report:

The direct fixing of wage rates implies the specific determination of the income of labor. It could in no event be acceptable unless coupled with direct and specific determination of the salaries of management, the dividends of stockholders, the interest payments received by bondholders, the incomes of farmers or merchants, of professional persons and of all others.

It should be noted that this statement on wages accompanied the Senate version of the bill, which contained a statement of policy that:

It shall be the policy of those departments and agencies of the government dealing with wages (here the bill names labor agencies) within the limits of their authority and jurisdiction, to work toward a stabilization of prices and cost of production.

It is clear therefore that the position of the committee did not encompass the establishment of wage controls.

In his own testimony Mr. Henderson, the Price Administrator, sharply differentiated between the policy of price control and any policy of wage control. In a portion of his testimony, part of which has been previously quoted, he said:

Wage control is quite a different thing from price control. It is really a control of income. It would be similar to profit control, in my opinion. (House Committee Hearings, p. 144)

3. Congress' Attitude on Wage Increases

It is clear from the legislative record that the Congress definitely anticipated that wage increases would continue to take place through collective bargaining and that such action was to be considered necessary and desirable.

First, by rejecting wage controls as recounted above, the Congress made clear that it did not wish to place restraints upon the increase of wages.

Secondly, the statements of the House and Senate leaders handling the bill make clear that they realized the necessity for wage increases.

For example, Mr. Williams, leading the House Committee's presentation of the bill, in his discussion of the wage provisions, specifically cited the fact that "the one unanswerable, irrefutable and conclusive proof that prices have not been increased in order to meet wage increases" is the profits made by the corporations during 1941.

Furthermore, he recognized that the past wage increases had been offset by the increased output per man-hour in industry. Such a conclusion of course assumes that further increases in output per man-hour should similarly be offset by further wage increases.

Similarly in the Senate in a statement on the matter of wages, Senator Prentiss Brown, there handling the bill, made a statement which speaks for itself as to the necessity of wage increases:

Wage adjustments in this country, as in Great Britain, should continue to be made through the normal processes of collective bargaining, assisted by the mediatory activities of the War Labor Board shortly to be established.

It is well known that as the rate of production increases in modern industry the labor costs per unit of output automatically decrease. This allows increased profits to be gained on each unit of output. The net profits of 416 large industrial corporations were about 30 per cent larger in the first 9 months of 1941 than in the first 9 months of last year.

These increases took place in spite of substantial wage increases in the early part of 1941, and in spite of substantially increased taxes. It would be most unfair, therefore, to take any measure freezing wages at this time. To do so would greatly enhance the already excessive profits of major industrial corporations at the expense of the working people.

In many places in this country wages are still being paid at rates below the level necessary to maintain workers at an American standard of living. It would be unwise to seek to prevent the necessary wage changes from taking place by the process of collective bargaining.

In addition to that matter, I will say that I, for one, feel that we ought to give full faith and credit to the effort of labor and management to get together. Labor, by public announcement, has given up the right to strike during the period of the emergency. Consequently, the mediation and conciliation services will be used for the purpose of settling wage disputes. There is no question but that if we freeze wages, if we freeze the cost of production, and since there is a great increase in the velocity of business caused by mass production, and so forth, industrial profits will inevitably rise. I am not at all unsympathetic with the desire and wish of those in control of the matter of wages to obtain a reasonable part of that joint product of capital and labor; and that subject, of course, needs consideration in connection with the inevitable rise in the cost of living which I am satisfied this bill cannot fully prevent.

In the third place, the Conference Committee itself in reconciling the views of the House and Senate Committees found it necessary to modify the statement of policy in such a way as to make clear the intent that wage adjustments should take place. This was done by adding the underlined phrase in the statement of policy on wages as follows:

> It shall be the policy of those agencies of the government dealing with wages . . . within the limits of their authority and jurisdiction, to work toward the stabilization of prices, *fair and equitable wages,* and cost of production.

This addition makes clear the Congress' concern that the statement of policy be not construed as preventing labor from obtaining fair and equitable wages.

In this connection it is important to read Senator Brown's statement which was made on behalf of the Senate Committee to the Senate even before the phrase "fair and equitable wages" was added to the policy statement. Senator Brown's discussion makes clear that it was not the intent of the Committee by this statement to freeze wages.

WAGE INCREASE AND INFLATION [8]

The wage increase of $1.00 a day should not be denied because of any fallacious argument that such wage increase will cause inflation.

The steel corporations may argue that they should be allowed to keep their excessive profits and refuse an equitable wage increase on the ground that such increase would be inflationary. If this argument is accepted in this case, it means that the wages for all wage earners throughout the nation are completely and absolutely frozen. In this case the S.W.O.C. (Steel Workers Organizing Committee) has fully justified its demand for a wage increase of $1.00 a day. If this demand is not granted in this case because of the fallacious inflationary argument, then no wage increase can possibly be obtained in any case.

The argument that the S.W.O.C. demand for wage increase should not be granted because of the threat of inflation is

[8] Steel Workers Organizing Committee, National War Labor Board. Brief submitted in the matter of Steel Workers Organizing Committee and Bethlehem Steel Company and others. p. 103-10. 1943.

fallacious and subversive of our Victory War Program. Our reasons are as follows:

1. The profit records of the four steel corporations show that the requested wage increase can be paid under the present price structure and out of present profits even if further increases in output per worker do not result. As we have shown in a previous portion of our brief, there can be reasonably anticipated further productive efficiency which will increase profits. Therefore the wage increases would not be inflationary in the sense of causing any justified price rise through rises in labor cost per unit which could not be absorbed in the present price structure.

2. Increased costs attributable to wage increases have not been primarily responsible for price rises either in the steel industry or in industry as a whole.

3. To cut purchasing power by freezing wages is inequitable and against sound public policy. Such a method of cutting first hits incomes which are already insufficient to maintain the worker in health and efficiency, and it hits them without regard to family circumstances.

The best known study on the amount of income necessary for workers was that of the Heller Committee of the University of California which indicated that a worker's family of five needed at least $2,211.00 for a reasonable minimum standard of living in San Francisco in March, 1941. Corrected to present day living costs, this standard would require more than $2,400.

In 1941, 69 per cent of American families received less than $2,000 and 34 per cent received less than $1,000. Of the workers in the plants under consideration, approximately two-thirds receive less than $2,000, the average wage for 1941 being approximately $1,900.

On medical care alone the need for such income is clearly illustrated. On such an income the usual family can spare only about $75 for medical care. The cost of adequate medical care for a family of four is over $300. It must also be recalled that out of these incomes workers are required to pay taxes. Even in 1939 families with incomes between $1,000 and $3,000 were paying approximately 17 per cent of their total income in various forms of taxation. The tax bill in 1941 added substantially to this burden.

To cut purchasing power of American people by freezing wages is most inequitable because it strikes primarily against incomes which, as is demonstrated above, were already insufficient to maintain the worker and his family in health and efficiency. It would mean that each new rise in the cost of living, 1 to 2 per cent a month, 10 to 20 per cent a year would be a direct flat tax upon all working people. No one has yet dared propose openly a flat tax of such magnitude, but the attempt to freeze wages at this time amounts to exactly the same thing.

Furthermore, the freezing of wages as a method of cutting purchasing power rests with equal heaviness [upon those] with high incomes who have no dependents and upon workers with lower incomes who have large families to support. It takes no cognizance of the difference in income requirements of various workers' families. Obviously in comparison with progressive income taxation the freezing of wages is a most inequitable and improper method of reducing purchasing power.

The freezing of wages would greatly damage the American Victory production effort, by damaging irreparably the health, efficiency and morale of American workers.

4. A sound public policy calls for the regulation of inflation first by effective price control on the prices that go into the cost of living; second by rationing all scarce goods; and third by cuts in purchasing power through progressive taxation and voluntary savings.

To undertake anti-inflationary measures by attempting first of all to freeze wages strikes first at the income of the lowest income groups and is quite the reverse of sound public policy. This is merely taking the step of supposed least resistance. Labor is ready and willing to accept its proper share of cuts in purchasing power if these are applied equitably by progressive taxation and by voluntary savings. But these cuts should come after the income of corporations has been equitably distributed as between owners and workers.

The fair and just way to meet the problems of inflation is through government controls equitably applied.

The first necessity is for effective control of the prices which go into the cost of living. As Mr. Leon Henderson said in his testimony to the House in August, 1941:

> It seems to me that one of the ways and the most important way to keep wages under control is to influence the cost of living by keeping prices in bounds. . . . To my mind the first approach to the wage needs, together with the supplemental approaches of other agencies, is through the cost of living basis.

In spite of this fact no clear attempt has been made by the Office of Price Control to put a brake on the prices which go into the rapidly rising cost of living of wage earners.

As long as the prices of the things that they buy are rising at the rate of 1 to 2 per cent a month, workers can ill afford to forego wage increases.

Some goods will become so scarce that it is necessary to ration. It seems to labor that a sound, thorough-going rationing system ought to be set up immediately. Commodities which are every day necessities and which become so scarce that there are not enough available to go around should be rationed promptly. This is the only fair way to prevent price increases on such goods and to see that everyone is provided according to his needs within the limit of supplies.

At the same time that these steps are taken, labor recognizes that it also becomes necessary during a period of increasing war production to reduce the amount of purchasing power which consumers are likely to spend. For reasons given above the freezing of wages is one of the worst possible ways to approach this task. It should be recognized that cuts in purchasing power go on in the normal economy through taxation and through savings. In the war economy these measures must be intensified. Labor readily agrees to that.

Only through taxation and voluntary saving can the cuts in purchasing power be made on that income that people do not need to buy the basic necessities of life. The taxation should be applied on a progressive or ability-to-pay basis so that the highest incomes are cut first. The incomes that are needed by working people to buy enough food, clothing and housing to maintain them in good health and full efficiency and high morale should be the last to be taxed. When such worker's income is taxed it means that the productive capacity of the nation is being reduced.

Only by a tax system with exemptions for dependents and based upon net income can the cuts in purchasing power be applied with some reasonable relationship to ability-to-pay and to family responsibility.

About 63 per cent of the usual worker's income goes to the purchasing of food, clothing and housing. A recent study made by the C.I.O. among workers who last year received wage increases showed that out of an increased expenditure of $21 in November, 1941 over November, 1940, $19 went to expenditures for food, clothing and housing.

As long as the nation can produce additional food, which it can, and additional clothing, which it can, and there are working people who need more food and clothing, it would be a dire mistake to prevent the increase of the incomes of such people.

5. In Great Britain wage adjustment is still carried on through the collective bargaining processes, even though that nation has been in the war over two years longer than the United States and the shortages in goods are much greater. Wage increases are still being granted both through collective bargaining and through the government tribunals. From the point of view of the national economy, the United States has much less reason for freezing wages than has Great Britain.

Mr. Leon Henderson summarized the situation in Great Britain in a memorandum presented to the House Committee on Banking and Currency September 17th, 1941 as follows:

> Wartime control of labor in Great Britain has operated within the framework of a settled government policy not to interfere with the voluntary negotiation of wage agreements. This policy first enunciated at the outbreak of war has been adhered to since in the midst of expanding government controls of economic life and despite a threatening inflationary situation.

The British government itself in a white paper on Price Stabilization and Industrial Policy, issued on July 22, 1941, set forth the policy as follows:

> It is the traditional and well tried practice of the principal industries to regulate wages through their joint voluntary machinery for wage negotiation. . . . Since the outbreak of war, the existing joint voluntary machinery for wage negotiations has operated successfully. Increases in wage rates have been reasonable; the authority of the unions in day-to-day adjustment of wages and conditions has been maintained; the freedom of opportunity to make claims and to have them discussed has enabled industrial peace to be maintained.
>
> The policy of the government, therefore, is to avoid modification of the machinery for wage negotiations and to continue to leave the various voluntary organizations and wage tribunals free to reach their decisions in accordance with their estimate of the relevant facts.

Wage rates in Great Britain have risen between 26 and 27 per cent since the beginning of the war. During the year 1941, while Great Britain was of course at war, aggregate increases of more than eight million dollars a week were made in the weekly full time wage rates of about 8 million workers.

The average increases in weekly earnings since the war began for British workers was 42 per cent. In metal engineering it was 49 per cent and in shipbuilding 73 per cent.

In the most important wage rate case decided in the last quarter of 1941 the National Arbitration Tribunal granted a wage increase of 5 shillings a week to more than two million workers in the metal working trades, including shipbuilding and machine manufacturing.

An examination of the *Ministry of Labour Gazette* reveals that wage increases are continuing throughout British industry both by the usual process of negotiation and by the awards of government tribunals.

Great Britain must of necessity import through the submarine blockade a very substantial part of its food and raw materials. It has been at war 2½ years. It reached practically full employment early last year. In contrast, the United States has been at war only 3 months. It still has great capacity for increasing its domestic food supply and its output of raw materials. It is a long way from reaching full employment of its labor force.

Therefore, in the United States there is far less ground for considering the freezing of wages than in Great Britain. And in Great Britain substantial wage increases are still being granted.

For these reasons the S.W.O.C. holds that it would be wholly improper and unsound to consider the danger of inflation as grounds for opposing the wage increase asked by S.W.O.C. in this case.

REPLY BRIEF [9]

Concerning wages as labor cost, there is a very considerable body of data. This data arose out of the discussion before Congressional committees on proposals for establishing wage control in connection with price control. Mr. Leon Henderson and Mr. Isador Lubin and their associates prepared extensive testimony to prove that up to the fall of 1941 such price increases as had taken place could not be attributed to wage increases.

The substance of the argument was two-fold; one, that an examination of price increases showed that as a matter of fact the price increases were of such a character that they could not be attributable to wage rises; and two, that the increased output per man-hour in industry due to the economies of increased operations were more than sufficient to pay for such wage increases as were granted.

The arguments made by Messrs. Henderson and Lubin with regard to the character of price increases in the fall of 1941 are still applicable. Neither they nor the companies have presented any testimony to prove that wage increases have yet, by increasing labor cost, required price increases.

Net profits of incorporated business, according to the national income figures of the Department of Commerce, for the year 1941 increased 31 per cent over 1940. The National City Bank of New York reports that the profits for 2,540 leading corporations for the year 1941 increased 20 per cent over 1940. The Federal Reserve Bank of New York also reports net profits for

[9] Steel Workers Organizing Committee, National War Labor Board. Reply brief submitted in the matter of Steel Workers Organizing Committee and Bethlehem Steel Company and others. p. 279-314. 1943.

1,128 corporations. These figures show an increase of 23.8 per cent in 1941 over 1940.

The vast majority of the companies could therefore grant wage increases now and have the additional cost come out of profits rather than increased prices, and do so without reducing profits below a reasonable level.

The argument now being made that all the benefits of increased productivity have been soaked up by past wage increases has not been proved. . . .

As far as industry in general is concerned, it would take some sharp reduction in the fantastic rise of industrial profits before taxes to create a convincing picture of costs rising to the point where price increases are justified. The union has already presented figures with regard to the corporations involved in this proceeding to show that, as far as they are concerned, the wage increases could easily be absorbed without bringing net profits down to levels which would justify the companies in asking increases in steel prices. This has also been demonstrated for the industry as a whole.

Another of Dr. Yntema's arguments was that, according to the figures of the Department of Commerce, the share of national income going to profits had not moved equitably with the share going to wages and salaries. In making this argument, Dr. Yntema compared profits after taxes with wages and salaries before taxes. A much fairer comparison, if such a comparison is useful, would be between profits before taxes and wages and salaries. The following table [p. 159] is offered to make this comparison; it makes clear that, as far as gross profits are concerned, they have recovered very substantially indeed in 1941 and represent a higher percentage of gross national product in 1941 than even in 1929. It further makes clear that with the rise of gross national product, profits have been rising at a more rapid rate than wages and salaries. . . .

The heavily increased burden of taxation to which corporations would be subject under the suggestions of the Secretary of the Treasury to the House Ways and Means Committee have been emphasized. The purpose of this exposition was apparently to imply that such increased taxation would, if passed, preclude wage increases.

PROFITS BEFORE TAXES

	National Product	*Profit Before Taxes*	*Wages and Salaries*	*Profits Before Taxes as Per cent of National Product*	*Wages and Salaries as Per cent of National Product*
1929........	97.4	8.7	52.2	8.9	53.6
1930........	86.2	1.6	47.4	1.9	55.0
1931........	70.5	—3.3	39.8	—4.7	56.5
1932........	53.9	—5.6	30.9	—10.4	57.4
1933........	52.9	—2.5	28.5	—4.7	53.9
1934........	61.6	0.1	32.4	—.16	52.6
1935........	69.0	1.7	35.4	2.5	51.4
1936........	79.5	4.4	39.6	5.5	49.8
1937........	86.1	4.4	44.6	5.1	51.7
1938........	80.0	1.6	41.1	2.0	51.4
1939........	86.3	4.3	44.3	5.0	51.3
1940........	94.3	6.4	48.2	6.8	51.2
1941........	114.7	11.5	61.2	10.2	53.4

This argument overlooks the fact that wages are a cost of production. Costs of production are subtracted from gross operating revenues and not from net profit. Therefore, in discussing the relation of wage costs to profits, the proper relation to consider is that between wage costs and gross profits, not net profits.

Inland Steel Company, for example, put considerable emphasis upon the fact that the Company was paying large taxes to the federal government. This fact was used in several ways. First, to prove that the net profit of the Company was decreasing as a result of increased taxation. Second, to show that in comparison with wages and tonnage output, the net profits (after taxes) had suffered. And third, that in the light of the proposed tax bill, the wage increases asked by S.W.O.C. (Steel Workers Organizing Committee) would, in fact, come from gross profits which would otherwise be paid to the United States Treasury in taxes.

These points imply that increases in wages should be governed by the character of federal tax policy. It assumes that, if it is the policy of the federal government to tax corporate profits, as well as individual income, unions should therefore not ask wage increases. It also argues that since the federal government plans to lay heavy taxes upon corporate income, and if the federal government needs such revenue, that therefore it is a sound public policy to build up high gross profits of corporations in order that they may provide the government with revenue. This concern to keep sufficient gross profits to provide the federal government with revenue implies that these companies will lend their support to heavy taxation upon industrial profits, which the position of the National Association of Manufacturers certainly repudiates.

The Treasury itself has never manifested concern that high industrial profits be kept in the hands of corporations in order that it may be more easily taxed. As a matter of fact, the Treasury's experience has been in recent years that even such increases of corporate taxes as it proposes are bitterly and effectively fought by American industry. So far no proposal of the Treasury for increased corporate taxation has been passed by the Congress without considerable changes which lighten the burden of taxes on the corporations. All the charts presented by the Inland Steel Company showing the probable tax liability for 1942 are based upon the highest brackets in the Treasury proposed corporate tax program. This assumes that the Congress will pass that tax program, an assumption unjustifiable by any previous experience in recent years. Even such moderate increases in corporate taxes as were suggested last year by the Treasury for the 1941 tax measure were not adopted by the Congress.

It would be interesting to know whether the National Association of Manufacturers is representing the views of the Inland Steel Company when it bitterly opposes the Treasury's suggestions for increased corporation taxes and asks instead the substitution of manufacturers' and retail sales taxes amounting to some 8 per cent. It seems fair to say that figures of the Inland Steel Company for its 1942 tax liability are pessimistically high. . . .

The second major aspect in which wage rises were discussed as an inflationary influence was the situation in which such increases would add to the excess of purchasing power over goods available for purchase. In developing this, Dr. Yntema made two major points: (1) that wage increases for the four steel firms involved, although not a serious addition to total purchasing power (some 44 million dollars as compared to a total of over 110 billion dollars for 1942), would actually set off wage increases for every worker in American industry; and (2) increasing war production will reduce the amount of goods available for consumer purchase while consumer income continues to mount. Such wage increases would be therefore an additional excess of purchasing power over goods available to consumers. . . .

There is no clear line of inevitability which makes wage increases in other industries always occur when such increases take place in steel. The wage increases which took place in the steel industry in the winter of 1936 were granted by the steel companies themselves in what proved to be a vain effort to forestall the organization of the steel industry by S.W.O.C. Furthermore, the steel companies increased the price of steel on an average of 3 to 5 dollars per ton. This steel price increase more than offset the increased cost to the steel companies of the wage increase. . . .

Also, the first major drive for organization in the mass production industries began in the steel industry, thus causing steel wages to increase first of all. The steel companies will hardly want to take credit for this circumstance. There was a general economic cause equally as important as the circumstances reported above. . . . The steel wage increases, both in 1937 and 1941, took place only after very rapid rises in steel output. Such rises in output were of course accompanied by substantially increased profits and prosperity in the steel industry.

Similarly, the general wage increases . . . took place as a result of well developed increases in general industrial prosperity. These increases, of course, parallel those of the steel industry. It is axiomatic in wage history that wage increases almost universally take place in periods of rising output and rising industrial prosperity. In this connection, it may be noted that since the period of the April, 1941 wage increase, the output, prosperity, and profits of the steel industry have continued to move upward with great acceleration. . . .

In an extensive technical article in the March, 1942, issue of the *Survey of Current Business,* Mr. Milton Gilbert, head of the National Income Section of the United States Department of Commerce, corrects the misapprehension that is created by using the national income figures rather than the figures of gross national product. Mr. Gilbert points out that one of the serious "sources of confusion concerning the impact of the war program upon the economic structure" has risen from inappropriate comparisons of war expenditures and national income. He then goes on. . . .

The total of war expenditures expressed as a percentage of national income, can be used to symbolize the general magnitude of the war effort, or its changes over time. However, the projected war program of 56 billion dollars frequently has been subtracted from a forecasted national income total for the fiscal year 1943, in the belief that the remainder would represent the output of goods and services available for civilian consumption. This remainder is then contrasted with one calculated for 1941 and a conclusion is drawn as to the extent of curtailment of consumption required to realize the war program.

For example, projected war expenditures of 56 billion dollars have been subtracted from an assumed national income total for fiscal 1943 of 110 billion, leaving a residual of 54 billion. In 1941, on the other hand, defense expenditures were 13.2 billion and national income 94.5 billion, leaving a comparable residual of 81.3 billion. It is then concluded that goods for consumers must be cut by a third if the real resources required for the war program are to be made available.

Mr. Gilbert then points out that, "Such a use of national income and war expenditures does not produce useful or significant results. It does not show the real character of the economic problem and cannot yield proper directives for economic policy. It does not show the disposition of the economic resources required for the fulfillment of the war program, the changes that are necessary in the structure of products, nor the nature of magnitude of the fiscal problem involved.

The reason is that the national income is a type of aggregate which is not strictly comparable with the total of war expenditures.

. . . Mr. Gilbert has also commented:

Just as inappropriate use of the national income concept can lead to misconceptions regarding the prospects for consumers' goods output, so it can lead to a vast exaggeration of the fiscal program needed to prevent inflation. Errors are common on both the supply and demand sides of this question. On the supply side, as has been pointed out earlier in this article, the quantity of consumers' goods likely to be available is often greatly underestimated by direct subtraction of war expenditures from national income.

On the demand side, several common pitfalls may be mentioned. The national income cannot be used as if it measured income in the hands of the consuming public. The measure of Income Payments to Individuals is the more appropriate concept for this purpose. Even with this measure, however, it should be kept in mind that the tax liabilities of individuals must be deducted to arrive at disposable income of consumers.

As to the magnitude of consumers' income in fiscal 1943, errors are frequent because of a failure to offset the leverage of war expenditures by the reduction of private capital formation which the war program required. The business funds that are made redundant through the limitation on investment possibilities thereby lose their income creating effect. By and large, this offset will come about automatically if plant and equipment investment is prevented by priority and allocation control. For the flow of investment funds into inventory purchasing, however, contraction is far from certain until direct controls of both inventory holdings and retail prices are instituted.

In calculating the volume of spending that is likely to reach the market it is also necessary, of course, to take account of individuals' savings out of disposable income. The amount of such saving will tend to increase substantially because of two factors. The first and most important will be the non-availability of durable goods usually purchased by consumers. It cannot be expected that the whole of the purchasing power not spent for such goods will be saved. However, the necessity of continuing payments on outstanding consumer debt at a time when new debt creation will be curtailed simply because sales are curtailed, will absorb a substantial amount of buying power. Consumer credit outstandings may decline by more than 4 billion dollars this year, and by as much as 3 billion during the coming fiscal year.

Nowhere does Dr. Yntema bring out the fact that a very large amount of the increased purchases made by consumers, and especially workers, in 1941 were made by going into debt either through installment buying or other borrowing. A large part of workers' incomes in 1942 and 1943 will be absorbed by paying for the purchases made in 1941 and before. For example, at the close of 1941 there was $9,943,000,000 in outstanding consumer debt. The consuming public owed 42 per cent of this debt to retail merchants, 28 per cent to intermediary financial agencies such as cash-loan agencies, commercial banks, etc., and 6 per cent to service creditors such as doctors, dentists, nurses, hospitals, etc.

Between 1940 and 1941 consumer debt increased almost $800 million, or a little over 8 per cent. The outstanding consumer debt in 1941 was 22.2 per cent greater than in 1929. According to an article entitled "Public and Private Debt in the United States, 1929-1940," in the November, 1941 *Survey of Current Business,* "All types of private debt were substantially lower in 1940 than in 1929 except for consumer debt, which was well above the 1929 level." In other words, between 1929 and 1940 corporate long and short term debt, as well as farm mortgages, urban real estate mortgages, individual and noncorporate long and short term debt all decreased, while consumer debt increased from a level of $8 billion in 1929 to a little over $9 billion in 1940 and almost $10 billion in 1941.

Although there are no precise figures available to show the amount of outstanding debt held by consumers at various income levels, there is some material which throws considerable light upon this question. In 1940, the National Bureau of Economic Research published a book by Blanche Bernstein on *The Pattern of Consumer Debt,* 1935-1936. This book shows the distribution of installment purchases of certain types of consumer durable goods by income classes. For example, it found that 86.7 per cent of the furniture purchased on the installment plan was bought by individuals with incomes less than $2,000 a year; that 74.3 per cent of the refrigerators, 90.8 per cent of the radios; and 80.2 per cent of all other electrical equipment so purchased was bought by this same income group.

A memorandum on the control of consumer credit as a factor in armaments production was prepared in May, 1941 by Mr. Rolph Nugent, Director of the Department of Consumer Credit Studies, Russell Sage Foundation, New York City. Mr. Nugent was also Consultant to the Advisory Commission to the Council of National Defense. This memorandum stated in part:

If we exclude families earning less than $500 a year, a class which is practically eliminated by virtue of its poverty from the market for new durable goods, the consumer market as a whole takes the form of a pyramid with large numbers of families earning low incomes at the bottom and with progressively smaller numbers of families earning progressively higher incomes as the top is approached. Although the incidence of purchases of consumers' durable goods increases with incomes, the bulk of the purchasers of new durable goods are nevertheless to be found in the modest income classes. Installment purchasers are even more heavily concentrated among relatively low-income classes.

Thus between 80 and 90 per cent of the outstanding consumer debt in 1941 was owed by individuals with incomes of less than $2,500 a year. Even though consumer durable goods, such as radios, furniture, automobiles, refrigerators, and other electrical equipment, will not be available in as great quantities as in former years for consumers to purchase, a great deal of the income of workers during 1942 will go toward repaying outstanding obligations previously incurred. It is also worthwhile to point out that during 1941 even those consumer goods industries which are now being shut down were creating vast inventories of goods, a large part of which are still in manufacturers', wholesalers' and retailers' hands. A substantial part of workers' purchasing power in 1942 can still go to the purchase of goods manufactured in 1941 and now in inventory.

Beyond the questionable validity of some of Dr. Yntema's figures and the arguments adduced therefrom S.W.O.C. holds that there is a very strong case to be made against freezing wages to prevent inflation. This case is based upon the following general principles:

1. That the maximum production effort can be attained only when workers and their families receive real income sufficient to maintain them in good health, full efficiency and high morale. This income should be the last to be impaired.

2. Wage freezing would cut those incomes first which are least able to bear reduction.

3. All of the increase in consumer income between 1941 and 1942 is expected to come in the income brackets above $2,500. Any reduction in purchasing power should first be applied to the incomes that have been increased and to the incomes that

are not needed to maintain minimum real income for the attainment of full production.

4. Increases in incomes below $2,500 are less inflationary than increases in incomes above, because they tend to go to the purchasing of items which are most likely to be plentiful.

5. Current price rises do not appear to come from competition of consumers for goods, but from speculation and profiteering.

6. The first measures needed to prevent inflation are strict price control and rationing to stop the rise in the cost of living and to distribute equitably any scarce goods. Any cuts in purchasing power which are necessary should follow the establishment of effective price control and rationing and be applied by general fiscal measures such as progressive taxation and savings. . . .

Wage freezing in a period when prices are rising rapidly and national income is moving upward means a cut in the real incomes of a group of Americans in the lower brackets of income.

The average weekly earnings of workers in manufacturing industries was $35.10 in January, 1942. If all these workers worked 52 weeks a year—and during 1942 a great percentage of them will not. They will be earning an average of $1,825 a year. Obviously such an income is insufficient to maintain the average wage earners' family at anything like the proper level of health and efficiency. If such an income is fixed in this period of rising prices and increasing taxation, it will be slashed most severely. . . .

By April, 1942, assuming a continued increase in the cost of living at present rates and passage of the Treasury's tax bill, it would be further reduced by $190. That is, if an income of $2,000 is frozen as of April, 1941, it will have fallen to a real income in terms of April, 1943, dollars of about $1,200 a year. If the sales tax proposal of the National Association of Manufacturers were to be enacted instead of the Treasury's proposal for income taxes, a further loss between April, 1942, and April 1943, of $160 might be expected. Thus, under such a supposition, the real income of $2,000 in April, 1941 would

DISTRIBUTION OF FAMILIES AND SINGLE CONSUMERS AND OF AGGREGATE INCOME RECEIVED, BY INCOME LEVELS, 1941 AND ESTIMATED 1942

	1941 calendar year				*1942 calendar year*			
	Families and single consumers		*Aggregate consumer income*		*Families and single consumers*		*Aggregate consumer income*	
Income levels	*Number (in thousands)*	*Per cent*	*Amount (in millions)*	*Per cent*	*Number (in thousands)*	*Per cent*	*Amount (in millions)*	*Per cent*
Under $500	4,089	9.5	$1,349	1.5	2,900	6.8	$1,044	1.0
$500 to $750	4,477	10.4	2,825	3.0	3,782	8.8	2,424	2.3
$750 to $1,000	4,563	10.6	3,997	4.3	4,571	10.7	4,142	4.0
$1,000 to $1,250	4,692	10.9	5,279	5.7	5,152	12.1	5,887	5.7
$1,250 to $1,500	4,907	11.4	6,699	7.2	4,607	10.8	6,314	6.1
$1,500 to $1,750	3,659	8.5	5,891	6.4	4,289	10.0	6,941	6.7
$1,750 to $2,000	2,798	6.5	5,120	5.5	3,166	7.4	5,848	5.7
$2,000 to $2,500	4,520	10.5	10,111	10.9	3,740	8.8	8,416	8.1
$2,500 to $3,000	2,755	6.4	7,439	8.0	2,863	6.7	7,759	7.5
$3,000 to $4,000	2,927	6.8	9,894	10.7	3,293	7.7	11,180	10.8
$4,000 to $5,000	1,507	3.5	6,554	7.1	1,793	4.2	7,886	7.6
$5,000 to $10,000	1,378	3.2	9,367	10.1	1,529	3.6	10,504	10.2
$10,000 and over	775	1.8	18,115	19.6	1,015	2.4	25,155	24.3
All levels	43,047	100.0	92,640	100.0	42,700	100.0	103,500	100.0

(Source: Research Division, Office of Price Administration, Consumer Income and Demand Section.)

be reduced to a real income of $1,040 in April, 1943, or a loss of nearly half.

The Office of Price Administration has prepared some very pertinent statistics on the distribution of income. These statistics give some indication as to the income picture for 1941 and 1942. [See table page 167]

It should be noted that the table is considered as preliminary by the Office of Price Administration. For instance, the total of income received by consumers for 1942 is estimated at $103.5 billion. It is now generally accepted that such income will be $110 billion or more. The picture presented, however, will not probably be substantially changed by the revised figures. The table shows that 78.3 per cent of all the families and single consumers (consumer units) received less than $2,500 in 1941. Nevertheless, this 78.3 per cent received only 44.5 per cent of the total consumers income. The estimates for 1942 show that there are expected to be 75.3 of all consumer units receiving less than $2,500 a year. And this 75.3 per cent would receive only 39.6 per cent of all consumers income. In short, the percentage of consumer income going to those with incomes less than $2,500 would be decreased nearly 5 per cent between 1941 and 1942.

By this estimate, total consumer income is shown to increase from $92.6 billion to $103.5 billion between 1941 and 1942, or an increase of 21.3 per cent. However, the income of those consumer units receiving less than $2,500 is shown to decrease by 4.4 per cent, while the income of those receiving $2,500 or more is shown to increase by 21.7 per cent. When the revised figures are prepared, the disproportion of the increase will be even greater. Such figures clearly show that the increase in consumer income can be expected, in the main, to go to those with incomes of over $2,500, very few of whom are wage earners' families. . . .

To propose then that the increased consumer income be shut off from those below $2,500 a year is simply not touching the income groups where the increase of consumer income really will occur. Furthermore, it should be pointed out that the incomes above $2,500 are much less severely affected by rises in the cost of living because much less a proportion of such incomes goes for the purchase of the commodities which constitute the basic cost of living. This is clearly shown by the material in the Consumer Expenditures study of the National Resources Committee. Less than 10 per cent of the employees covered by this proceeding earned more than $2,500 in 1941 and their increased incomes resulting from the dollar-a-day are being taxed more.

It is sound public policy to apply whatever cuts in purchasing power may be necessary to the group of incomes above $2,500 before applying it to those below $2,500. The wage earner groups are, in the main, below $2,500. Any wage freezing proposal would strike at these first.

The consumers in the lower income groups spent the largest part of their incomes on necessities. Most workers spent from 60 to 70 per cent of their incomes on food, clothing and rent. Between 30 and 40 per cent goes to the purchase of food. As the family income increases, the percentage going for the basic necessities decreases. The most elaborate study on this problem made by the National Resources Committee sets forth this situation in great detail.

PERCENTAGE OF INCOME OF AMERICAN FAMILIES FOR MAIN CATEGORIES OF CONSUMPTION, BY INCOME LEVEL, 1935-36

Income level	*Food*	*Housing*	*Household Operation*	*Clothing*
Under $500	65.0	28.9	18.2	11.2
$500 to $750	49.5	19.9	13.5	8.9
$750 to $1,000	43.5	18.5	12.1	8.9
$1,000 to $1,250	38.7	18.1	11.6	8.9
$1,250 to $1,500	35.7	16.9	10.9	9.0
$1,500 to $1,750	32.7	16.6	10.3	9.1
$1,750 to $2,000	30.5	16.5	10.2	9.0
$2,000 to $2,500	27.8	15.7	9.6	9.3
$2,500 to $3,000	25.4	14.9	9.6	9.4
$3,000 to $4,000	22.7	14.3	9.4	9.3
$4,000 to $5,000	19.4	13.0	9.1	9.3
$5,000 to $10,000	15.1	11.4	8.5	8.1
$10,000 to $15,000	10.7	10.6	6.7	7.3
$15,000 to $20,000	10.3	8.6	6.8	7.3
$20,000 and over	5.4	6.5	5.2	5.2
All levels	28.8	24.4	10.0	8.7

(Consumer Expenditures in the United States, National Resources Committee, 1939, Table 6A, page 78)

Furthermore, the families in the lower income groups spent most of their money for the type of goods and services which can be substantially expanded. It is widely accepted that there is expected to be no shortage of basic foods in the United States except for certain types of imported commodities such as sugar and coffee. The opportunities for additional expenditure in the lower income groups for medical care and recreation and for other such services is not seriously limited.

. . .[In] the study on "Consumer Expenditures in the United States," it is pointed out in some detail that in the lower income groups below $2,500, reductions in income, that is, real income, cut directly into food, housing and clothing in almost direct proportion to the reduction in income. In the upper income brackets such reductions in income do not necessarily reduce the expenditures on basic necessities, but tend to reduce expenditures for luxuries or for semi-luxury durable goods. Such durable goods are the items which are being most severely cut in supply at the present time. . . .

Wholesale prices and prices in the primary markets have led retail price increases by a remarkable extent in almost all commodities. This leads to the suggestion that it is not the active competition of the consumer such as wage earners for goods which has been the moving factor in the price rises, but instead speculative anticipations on the part of merchants in the primary markets which have set off the major price increases.

There seem to be no clear signs in any of the major commodities of bidding up prices at retail or consumer levels. In fact, for a very large number of the commodities upon which prices have been raised there were extensive inventories in the hands of manufacturers, wholesalers and retailers. The price rises appear instead to have been, then, the result of expectation that such prices could be gotten rather than an actual competition by consumers for the goods.

In the Temporary National Economic Committee hearings on the Investigation of Concentration of Economic Power, Part 21, *War and Prices,* Mr. Leon Henderson, Dr. Lubin and others discussed extensively the prices and hourly wage situation in the First World War. Two comments made there are worth while noting:

> Mr. Henderson: Going back to some of your other charts on prices, for example, bituminous coal, textiles, iron and steel, did these increases in hourly rates and weekly earnings absorb all of the price rise in that period?
>
> Dr. Lubin: What do you mean by that?
>
> Mr. Henderson: Is the price rise in textiles and coal and iron and steel to be accounted for solely by the increase (in wages)?
>
> Dr. Lubin: No; the proof of that fact is, you see, these prices went much higher. Wages did go up, but nowhere near enough in many instances to make up for the increase in the cost of living. In other words, there was a shortage so far as labor was concerned. He was not getting back the difference. You could not say that his wage increases were responsible for those prices because after he got his wage increases he could not get as much for his money as he formerly got.

Further on, Dr. Willard Thorp, in discussing the kind of demand that led to wholesale price increases, said:

> I think Dr. Lubin has indicated the fact that there was no tremendous purchasing on the part of consumers, at least not by government employees and wage earners. The demand was quite a different sort of demand as you indicated and not so much a demand for consumers goods as it was for the heavier types of things which are used more directly in prosecuting a war.

These expert statements speak for themselves.

Economists in this country and abroad have until recently had little experience with the problems of controlling inflation. It has been theoretically considered by some that reductions in purchasing power roughly equal to the excess of purchasing power over goods available must take place before price control and rationing can become effective. . . .

Certain economists, however, in examining the British and German experience in particular have come to a different conclusion which appears to have considerable validity. It is in fact the conclusion that has been set forth by leaders of labor, namely, that the first steps toward the effective control of inflation must be strict price control on commodities which go into the cost of living in particular, and an extensive rationing system on all commodities of which there is a real or artificial shortage.

Apparently, it has been the experience abroad, first, that most prices rise not as a direct result of increased purchasing power but in anticipation of the creation of increased purchasing power. Secondly, that attempts to reduce purchasing power first are not effective as a device for preventing price rises in wartime. Thirdly, it is possible effectively to reduce consumer purchasing power only after real price control and rationing have been instituted, and then much of the excess consumer purchasing power automatically goes into savings, or is otherwise withdrawn from the market.

A very interesting monograph on this issue has been prepared in the Department of Commerce. (*Rationing,* by Arthur R. Upgren and Richard M. Bissell, Jr., Division of Research and Statistics, Department of Commerce, March 12, 1942.)

The following excerpts are pertinent. In reading these it should be recalled that wage freezing is a form of fiscal measure to reduce purchasing power:

In the abstract the problem of coping with an impending inflation is simple. The weapons consist of taxation, the borrowing power, and perhaps, the power to compel saving. Yet, despite the universal agreement upon the efficacy of these devices for preventing inflation, recent evidence from the experience of other countries reveals that the problem is never, in fact, solved in this way. Rather, the weight of the evidence (especially from Britain and Germany) is in support of the view that the major and primary responsibility for the avoidance of inflation falls upon those endowed with the power of rationing. This they may not like, and it is not intended to suggest that fiscal policy can not and should not supplement the activities of the rationers but they must recognize that they can and probably will perform this function. When the power to control prices is granted, and when the difficulties in the way of developing an adequate fiscal policy are so great, only effective broad use of the power to ration can create the conditions necessary for effective price control.

There is yet to be provided a convincing case of any country in war adopting fiscal policies in the degree necessary to maintain anything approaching substantial stability in prices. In contrast there is considerable evidence that reasonably satisfactory fiscal measures can be adopted *only if* those empowered to ration have first done their job well.

This statement rests upon the evidence that whatever stability of prices has been attained in Germany and Britain, for example, has been secured far more through effective use of the rationing weapon than by fiscal measures. In fact such fiscal measures probably could not have been as effective as they may have been except for the prior exercise of rationing powers. Stated in another way, dictatorships no less than democracies have found the imposition of an adequate fiscal policy, initially, almost impossible unless there was first created by rationing an excess of idle purchasing power.

In Germany, with a government of great and effective centralized control, only 50 per cent of the war budget has been raised by taxation. In Britain, the figure is but 27 per cent. At the moment we are about halfway between these extremes. Yet relative to the price development in the United States, the price level in Britain and Germany has been reasonably well controlled under financial conditions much more explosive than has been the case for the United States. With their prior imposition of widespread rationing there has been *first* created idle funds which subsequently have been tapped by the government sales of bonds that have reasonably well mopped up such surplus purchasing power.

Proponents of a frontal attack upon general inflation by fiscal policy must recognize the extreme difficulty of first restricting purchasing power at a time when goods are still reasonably free in supply and still free to move in price because neither rationing nor price control has been widely used. But the use of the power to ration can check the supplies of goods and the use of power to control prices can further aid in reducing the stream of spending. In this way is created a surplus of purchasing power for which immediate and customary use channels are not open. As a result the consumer far more willingly acquiesces in the drive of government to secure these funds; when his ordinary alternatives, even at rising prices, are available to him he remains an unwilling subject or accomplice.

EXCERPTS

Wage increases, given with full ability of companies to pay, are not in themselves inflationary. They would be inflationary only if workers spent them in such a way as to break price ceilings and force prices upward. Inflation is not caused by the income people receive. It can be caused by inflationary spending, but this is an entirely different matter and can be controlled by special measures. It is significant that even if wage increases this year equal last year's volume, they would amount to less than one-fifth of the entire increase in consumer spending power in 1942. Actually wage increases so far in 1942 have been much less than 1941.—*American Federation of Labor. Proceedings,* 1942. *p.* 119-20.

I rise to speak a word of commendation of Mr. William Green, president of the American Federation of Labor, and of Mr. Philip Murray, president of the Congress of Industrial Organizations. It is reported in this morning's papers that, instead of asking the President to raise wages, they have asked him to lower prices.

Their request is a just one. They have, in effect, asked that the principles embodied in the Price Control Act of October 2, 1942, for the stabilization of wages and prices, be adhered to and rigidly enforced.

Mr. Green is quoted in the Washington Post as saying:

If wage stabilization is to be part of this program, price stabilization must be parallel.

In those words he expressed the very essence and purpose of the Price Control Act.—*Charles S. Dewey, Representative from Illinois. Congressional Record. Ap.* 2, '43. *p.* A1692.

At its last meeting in Washington at the end of March, the C.I.O. Executive Board unanimously adopted a resolution calling upon you as Price Administrator to establish immediately effective price control on the commodities going into the cost of living. It further called upon you to establish immediately fair and equitable systems in rationing. I am enclosing a copy of this resolution for your information.

The workers of this country are suffering an increasingly unbearable burden because of the failure of the Price Administration to institute effective price control and rationing. Within the past year, workers' cost of living has risen 15 and 20 per cent, with even the Bureau of Labor Statistics index for the cost of living for big cities rising over 13 per cent. You well know that unless effective steps are taken immediately this cost of living will continue to rise at least at the rate of the past year.

These rises in the cost of living are cuts in workers' wages. They mean less food, housing and clothing for the men and women in the war plants who are turning out the weapons of victory. These wage cuts mean that the health, the efficiency and the morale of our war production workers are being seriously impaired and the war production will suffer accordingly. It is your responsibility to stop these price rises.

In May, 1940, this responsibility was conferred upon you in the Price Division of the National Defense Advisory Commission. In April, 1941 authority was conveyed to you by executive order to deal with prices through a new Office of Price Administration and Civilian Supply. On January 30, 1942, additional authority was placed in your hands by the approval of the Emergency Price Control Act. Among the purposes set forth for this act were "to stabilize prices and to prevent speculative, unwarranted, and abnormal increases in prices and rents, . . . to protect persons with relatively fixed and limited incomes, consumers, wage earners . . . from undue impairment of their standard of living."

As yet, no effective action to control the cost of living has been taken under these authorities and the working people of the country are suffering intensely thereby.

Efforts have been made to camouflage this failure behind the smokescreen of an attack upon labor, implying that the increases in the cost of living have been due to the wages of labor. This is false and you well know it to be. There has been no general wage rate increase in any basic industry since the spring of last year. Therefore the price rises which have been taking place cannot be blamed on labor's wages.

The wage adjustments now under negotiation are required to offset in part the damage already done to workers' living standards by the tremendous rises in the cost of living over the past year. They are required also to protect workers and their families against rises that clearly cannot be prevented even by immediate price control action. This nation has certainly not reached the point where it must break down the level of livelihood that is needed to keep its working people in health and efficiency.

I am writing you this letter to plead with you to institute immediately an effective and widespread system of price control upon the prices of the goods that people need to buy in order to live. I am urging you to establish the widespread rationing system that may be necessary to implement price control. I make this plea in the name of production for victory, for without effective price control and rationing our Victory Production Program will be woefully impaired.

Proper price control and rationing require the participation of representatives of labor in its administration so that full cognizance may be taken of that large body of Americans so adversely affected by price increases. You may be assured that labor will cooperate to the fullest in the establishment of the price control and rationing measures necessary to bring cost of living under control.—*Letter by Philip Murray, President, C.I.O., to Price Administrator Leon Henderson, April* 6, 1942. *Brief submitted in the matter of Steel Workers Organizing Committee and Bethlehem Steel Company and others. Appendix J.* 1943.

BIBLIOGRAPHY

An asterisk (*) preceding a reference indicates that the article or a part of it has been reprinted in this book.

BIBLIOGRAPHIES

Summers, Robert E., comp. Wages and prices. p. 207-19. (Reference Shelf. Vol. 15, no.6) H.W. Wilson Co. N.Y. Ap. '42.

United States. Library of Congress. Division of Bibliography. Inflation: a supplementary list of references. Florence S. Hellman, comp. 43p. mim. Wash. D.C. Ja. 29, '43.

BOOKS AND PAMPHLETS

*American Federation of Labor. Report of proceedings, 1942. p. 214-21. Labor Policy Committee of OPA. The Federation. Wash. D.C.

P. 217-18. A. F. of L.'s anti-inflation program; also reprinted in Congressional Record. 88:A2140. Jl. 23, '42.

Anderson, Kurt, comp. Salary stabilization under the jurisdiction of the Commissioner of Internal Revenue. 51p. processed. C.I.S. Publication no.44) Current Information Service. 5926 Kensington Rd. Detroit, Mich. '43.

Anderson, Kurt, comp. Wage and salary stabilization under the jurisdiction of the National War Labor Board. 68p. processed. (C.I.S. Publication no.43) Current Information Service. 5926 Kensington Rd. Detroit, Mich. '42.

Chamber of Commerce of the State of New York. Control of inflation; resolutions and report. 9p. The Chamber. N.Y. O. '42.

Clark, John M. How to check inflation. 31p. (Pamphlet no.64) Public Affairs Committee. 30 Rockefeller Plaza. N.Y. '42.

Gill, Norman N. Report on salary and wage trends in various cities. 17p. mim. Municipal Reference Library. City Hall. Milwaukee, Wis. '41.

Katona, George. War without inflation; the psychological approach to problems of war economy. 213p. Columbia Univ. Press. N.Y. '42.

Kemmerer, Edwin Walter. ABC of inflation; with particular reference to present-day conditions in the United States. 174p. Whittlesey House. N.Y. '42.

Especially Chap. 7, Inflation and wages.

Kjellstrom, Erik T. H. and others. Price control; the war against inflation. 171p. Rutgers University Press. New Brunswick, N.J. '42.

Nourse, Edwin G. Wages as cost and as market. 43p. (Pam. no.44) Brookings Institution. Wash. D.C. '42.
Chapter 9 of his forthcoming book Price Making in a Democracy.

Procedure and preparation of cases before the National War Labor Board. 72p. Congress of Industrial Organizations. 718 Jackson Pl. Wash. D.C. D. '42.

*Seward, Ralph T.; Porter, Paul R.; and Lapham, Roger D. Wage stabilization and adjustment. 28p. (Personnel series no.61) American Management Association. 330 W. 42d St. N.Y. '42.

*Steel Workers Organizing Committee. National War Labor Board: [Brief submitted] in the matter of Steel Workers Organizing Committee and Bethlehem Steel Company, Republic Steel Corporation, Youngstown Sheet & Tube Company, Inland Steel Company; with reply brief. 348p. United Steelworkers of America. 1500 Commonwealth Bldg. Pittsburgh, Pa. '43.

Steiner, George A. ed. Economic problems of war. v.p. John Wiley & Sons. N.Y. '42.
See Index.

*Stewart, Bryce M. Some major aspects of wage and manpower controls. 20p. typew. The Author. Industrial Relations Counselors, Inc. 1270 6th Av. N.Y. Mr. 9, '43.

Stewart, Bryce M. Wage and manpower controls in Canada. 16p. (Personnel Management series no.59) American Management Association. 330 W. 42nd St. N.Y. '42.

Summers, Robert E., comp. Wages and prices. 219p. (Reference Shelf. Vol. 15, no.6) H.W. Wilson Co. N.Y. '42.

United States. Senate. Committee on Banking and Currency. Stabilizing the cost of living; hearings September 15-16, 1942 on S.J. Res.161. 250p. 77th Cong. 2d sess. Supt. of Doc. Wash. D.C. '42.

Wages in manufacturing industry in the United States. 55p. Statistical Department. National Association of Manufacturers. 14 W. 49th St. N.Y. N. '41.

PERIODICALS

Academy of Political Science. Proceedings. 20:11-22. My. '42. Problems of price control. J. M. Clark.

Academy of Political Science. Procedings. 20:23-34. My. '42. Price and wage control in Canada. A. F. W. Plumptre.

*Academy of Political Science. Procedings. 20:79-86. My. '42. Labor's view of wage policies from now on. James B. Carey.

American Economic Review. 32:744-59. D. '42. Price control in outline. Don D. Humphrey.

American Federationist. 48:8. N. '41. Wage freezing is opposed.

American Federationist. 49:16-17. Je. '42. Wage increases.

American Federationist. 49:18-19+. Je. '42. Price control, rationing and organized labor. Leon Henderson.

American Federationist. 49:3-5+. Ag. '42. Wages and inflation. Boris Shishkin.

American Federationist. 49:18. Ag. '42. Keep collective bargaining.

*American Federationist. 49:4-5+. O. '42. Cold facts about wages.

American Forum of the Air. 4, no.16:3-14. Ap. 19, '42. Should we freeze all prices and wages for the duration? Claude Pepper and others.

American Forum of the Air. 4, no.30:3-15. S. 20, '42. We discuss the President's Labor Day message. Henry Cabot Lodge, Jr. and others.

American Mercury. 55:66-71. Jl. '42. Inflation and you. Ludwig von Mises.

American Statistical Association. Journal. 37:377-82. S. '42. Prices and wages. Walter G. Keim.

Annals of the American Academy. 224:58-61. N. '42. Should wages be frozen? William Green.

*Annals of the American Academy. 224:62-8. N. '42. Wage adjustments in this war. Z. Clark Dickinson.

Annals of the American Academy. 224:75-83. N. '42. War labor policies in Canada. Margaret Mackintosh.

Annals of the American Academy. 224:88-95. N. '42. Democratic obligations of management and labor in total war. Carroll R. Daugherty.

Annals of the American Academy. 224:141-6. N. '42. Aims and policies of the National War Labor Board. William H. Davis.

Atlantic Monthly. 170:sup. 25-6. Ag. '42. What about inflation? James B. Carey and Leroy A. Lincoln.

Atlantic Monthly. 170:29-30. S. '42. Wages and inflation. William Green.

Atlantic Monthly. 170:29-30. O. '42. How to stop inflation. William P. Witherow.

*Atlantic Monthly. 171:74-82. Ja. '43. How much trade-unionism as usual? Sumner H. Slichter.

Baltimore. 36:19-22. D. '42. Wage and salary control. Ernest L. Martin.

Barron's. 22:4. My. 4, '42. New Dealers think anti-inflation program insufficient, and expect further moves. Edson Blair.

Barron's. 22:4-5. My. 11, '42. President's anti-inflation program not being put into force on important sectors. Edson Blair.

Barron's. 22:4-5. Jl. 13, '42. President continues to quarter-back domestic issues. Edson Blair.

Barron's. 22:3. O. 19, '42. Price-wage control bullish for stocks. Barnett Ravits.

Barron's. 22:3-4. N. 9, '42. Your new taxes; revolutionary new salary measure. Lionel J. Freeman.

Correction. Barron's. 22:7. N. 16, '42.

Barron's. 23:4. F. 8, '43. Stabilization Director Byrnes plans strong fight against inflation. Edson Blair.

Barron's. 23:4+. F. 15, '43. Lewis forces a showdown on inflation program. Edson Blair.

Barron's. 23:3. Mr. 15, '43. Lewis fights for inflation. Stanley G. Thompson.

Business Week. p. 88. Ap. 11, '42. What a freeze really means.

Business Week. p. 34+. Ap. 25, '42. How Britain fights inflation.

Business Week. p. 41+. My. 9, '42. How Canada did it.

Business Week. p. 15-16. My. 23, '42. Wage policy, piecemeal.

Business Week. p. 76. Je. 6, '42. Needed: a triple play on labor.

Business Week. p. 16-17. Jl. 11, '42. Wage inflation? War Labor Board weighs its Little Steel decision.

Business Week. p. 78-9. Jl. 18, '42. OPA on wages; a definition of policy that curbs labor.

Business Week. p. 84-5. Ag. 15, '42. Pay ceiling: 15%; NWLB wants cost-of-living formula, set in Little Steel case, to be established as yardstick for all pay boosts.

Business Week. p. 20. Ag. 29, '42. Wage issue boils.

Business Week. p. 82. O. 31, '42. First rulings on wage freeze.

Business Week. p. 16. N. 14, '42. Oct. 15 pay base.

Business Week. p. 120+. N. 21, '42. Pay hike formula; NWLB all set to adjust salaries and wages.

Business Week. p. 56+. N. 28, '42. Wages and prices; if NWLB grants a boost in pay, then what happens to ceilings? OPA gives answer.

Business Week. p. 60+. D. 5, '42. NWLB's equalizer; additional wage rules include permission to narrow differentials between men's and women's pay.

Business Week. p. 86+. D. 19, '42. Escalator brake; NWLB clamps a lid on wage increases.

Business Week. p. 13. D. 26, '42. Price worries blur the future.

Business Week. p. 15-16. D. 26, '42. Appeasement on prices.

Canadian Chartered Accountant. 41:87-96. Ag. '42. Today's business; the control of prices and wages in Canada. John W. Love.

Christian Century. 59:653. My. 20, '43. Are war workers overpaid?

Commerce (Chicago) 39:15-16+. S. '42. Inflation and the war economy. John K. Langum.

Commercial and Financial Chronicle. 155:1345. Ap. 2, '42. Selfish demands of labor for wages, hours hit, as periling our existence.

Commercial and Financial Chronicle. 155:2121+. Je. 4, '42. Criticizes competitive bidding up of wages & salaries as forcing inflation. Marriner S. Eccles.

Commercial and Financial Chronicle. 156:372. Jl. 30, '42. Wage increase of 5.5 per cent authorized in Little Steel case—five guiding principles adopted.

Commercial and Financial Chronicle. 156:373. Jl. 30, '42. AFL head maps plan to control inflation. William Green.

Commercial and Financial Chronicle. 156:375. Jl. 30, '42. NWLB orders stabilization of wages in nine New England textile plants.

Commercial and Financial Chronicle. 156:889, 896-7. S. 19, '42. President demands stabilization of wages and profits, with new ceiling on farm products.

Commercial and Financial Chronicle. 156:1089+. S. 24, '42. Anti-inflation bills fail purpose and create vicious circle. William P. Witherow.

Commercial and Financial Chronicle. 156:1093+. S. 24, '42. Congress debates wage-price stabilization bills; President opposes higher parity formula.

Commercial and Financial Chronicle. 156:1094. S. 24, '42. Wages of many workers gives bare subsistence.

Commercial and Financial Chronicle. 156:1265+. O. 8, '42. Text of executive order providing for stabilizing wages, salaries, farm prices, etc.

Commercial and Financial Chronicle. 156:1267. O. 8, '42. Anti-inflation bill gives President broad powers over prices, wages, salaries; text of bill.

Same. Federal Reserve Bulletin. 28:1080-2. N. '42.

Commercial and Financial Chronicle. 156:2061. D. 10, '42. WLB jurisdiction to cover wage disputes in non-war industries.

Commercial and Financial Chronicle. 156:2069. D. 10, '42. NWLB policy outlined for wage increases.

Communist. 22:229-39. Mr. '43. Some problems of economic stabilization. Gil Green.

Conference Board Management Record. 4:363-4. N. '42. Wages and salary stabilization; main provisions of eleven general orders. E. S. Horning.

Conference Board Management Record. 4:395-7. D. '42. Changes in wages. Robert A. Sayre.

Congressional Digest. 21:195+. Ag. '42. Is the administration's present policy effective in preventing the rise of inflation? with pro and con discussion.

Congressional Digest. 22:19-32. Ja. '43. History and status of the proposed $25,000 salary limit.

Congressional Record. 88:3805-7. Ap. 27, '42. Message to Congress. Franklin D. Roosevelt.

*Congressional Record. 88:7283-5. S. 7, '42. Message to Congress. Franklin D. Roosevelt.

Same. New York Times. p. 14. S. 8, '42; United States Senate. Committee on Banking and Currency. Stabilizing the cost of living; hearings, September 15 and 16, 1942 on S.J.Res. 161. p. 1-6. 77th Cong. 2d sess. '42; *Condensed.* Bankers Magazine. 145:281-2. O. '42.

Controller. 10:571-3+. D. '42. How inflation is being fought in Canada. T. J. Monty.

Current History. n.s. 2:198-204. My. '42. Why the anti-labor drive? Ralph Volney Harlow.

Current History. n.s. 3:81-8. O. '42. Campaign against inflation. J. Donald Kingsley.

Current History. n.s. 3:191-9. N. '42. Stabilizing the home front. J. Donald Kingsley.

Eastern Underwriter. 43:38-9. pt. 2. O. 9, '42. Salary and wage control in Canada. Edward E. Duckworth.

Federal Reserve Bulletin. 28:1065-7. N. '42. Economic stabilization controls and war finance.

Federal Reserve Bulletin. 28:1080-5. N. '42. Emergency price control; text of act.

Fortune. 26:60-1+. Jl. '42. General Max over the U.S.; price ceilings. John Davenport.

Fortune. 26:75-9. Ag. '42. Lost $40 billion; more flowing into high salaries, but most of the pressure on prices is coming from those with $5,000 and less.

Fortune. 26:122-3+. O. '42. Washington fiscal policy: its war and postwar aims. Gerhard Colm and G. M. Alter.

Fortune. 26:100-2+. N. '42. What's itching labor? summary of opinion of workers in Pittsburgh area.

Fortune. 27:78-81+. Mr. '43. Inflation can still be checked.

Harvard Business Review. 20, no. 4:402-5. [Jl.] '42. Wage-setting dilemma. C. Canby Balderston.

Inland Printer. 110:27-8. Ja. '43. Experience of last four years teaches Canada that changes are necessary in price control setup. Kenneth R. Wilson.

International Labour Review. 45:125-41. F. '42. Consumer spending, inflation and the wage earner in the United States. Otto Nathan.

International Labour Review. 46:79-83. Jl. '42. Wage regulation and the incidence of the higher cost of living in Sweden.

International Labour Review. 46:489-91. O. '42. Wage stabilization in the United States.

International Labour Review. 47:383-5. Mr. '43. Development of wage policy in the United States.

Journal of Educational Sociology. 16:266-72. Ja. '43. National economic policy and the control of inflation. A. H. Feller.

Journal of Political Economy. 51:1-11. F. '43. Toward a national wartime labor policy: the wage issue. E. B. McNatt.

Labor's Monthly Survey (American Federation of Labor). 3:4-6. My. '42. Wage stabilization.

Magazine of Wall Street. 71:12-13+. O. 17, '42. Is inflation stopped? what the new controls can and can not do. Ward Gates.

Monthly Labor Review. 54:843-68. Ap. '42. Labor in transition to a war economy. Witt Bowden.

Monthly Labor Review. 55:466-72. S. '42. Canadian wage and cost-of-living order of July 1942.

Monthly Labor Review. 55:484-97. S. '42. Decisions of National War Labor Board, January-July 1942.

Monthly Labor Review. 55:903-12. N. '42. Indirect price increases. Melville J. Ulmer.

Monthly Labor Review. 55:917-24. N. '42. Stabilization of cost of living by wage and price control.

Monthly Labor Review. 55:1142-7. D. '42. Regulations controlling wage adjustments.

Monthly Labor Review. 56:59-67. Ja. '43. Decisions of National War Labor Board, August and September 1942.

Monthly Labor Review. 56:148-52. Ja. '43. Delegation of wage-approval power by War Labor Board.

Nation. 154:532-3. My. 9, '42. Wages and inflation.

Nation. 155:43-4. Jl. 18, '42. Should wages be frozen?

Nation. 156:185-6. F. 6, '43. Farm prices and wages.

*National City Bank of New York (Economic Conditions). p. 27-9. Mr. '42. New wage demands; the inflationary spiral.

*National City Bank of New York (Economic Conditions). p. 110-12. O. '42. Need of stronger control measures; three inflationary periods.

National City Bank of New York (Economic Conditions). p. 26. Mr. '43. Labor and the Little Steel formula.

National Municipal Review. 31:249-53. My. '42. Canada regulates wages, prices.

National Petroleum News. 34:33-5. O. 21, '42. Rules on anti-inflation and economic stabilization; complete text.

Nation's Schools. 30:20-1. S. '42. War salaries; can educational employes afford the luxury of war-time salary adjustments that widen unpopular inflationary gap? Lionel De Silva.

New Masses. 43:6-8. My. 19, '42. Should wages be frozen. A. B. Magil.

New Masses. 44:10-12. S. 15, '42. Ceilings Henderson must hit. Bruce Minton.

New Republic. 106:415-16. Mr. 30, '42. Ceilings against inflation.

*New Republic. 107:7-9, 18-19. Jl. 6, '42. Wages and arguments; with editorial comment. Harold J. Ruttenberg.

New Republic. 107:103-4. Jl. 27, '42. Wages and the war effort.

New Republic. 107:170-1. Ag. 10, '42. Record of the WLB.

*New Republic. 107:285-7. S. 7, '42. Unions, wages and inflation. Harold Mager.

New Republic. 108:180. F. 8, '43. Price-control problem.

New Republic. 108:273-6. Mr. 1, '43. Farmers, labor and prices. George Soule.

New York Herald Tribune. Sec. 2. p. 2. F. 28, '43. Roosevelt 48-hour-week order is called directly inflationary. Mark Sullivan.

New York State Education. 30:44-7+. O. '42. Teachers and the national welfare; inflation: the hidden pay cut. Alvin C. Eurich.

*New York Times. p. 14. F. 24, '43. Offer wage plan for electricians.

New York Times. p. 12. Mr. 6, '43. Retroactive wage increases.

New York Times. p. 6E. Mr. 28, '43. Demand for wage rises fought as inflationary. Louis Stark.

New York Times. p. 8E. Mr. 28, '43. NWLB set-up defended; with editorial comment. Roger D. Lapham and others.

Newsweek. 19:29. Je. 22, '42. WLB wage policy slowly takes shape. Ernest K. Lindley.

Newsweek. 20:52. Jl. 6, '42. That $1 a day; WLB hearings on Little Steel.

Newsweek. 20:48. Jl. 13, '42. Crucial test on wage and labor policy.

Newsweek. 20:46+. Jl. 27, '42. WLB sets up wage yardstick and evokes cry of inflation.

Newsweek. 20:50. Ag. 3, '42. Why the President cannot stop inflation. Ralph Robey.

Newsweek. 20:46+. Ag. 31, '42. Meat shortage ills are traced to booming purchasing power; how labor's wages interlock with farm prices.

Newsweek. 20:56+. N. 9, '42. What about raises?

Newsweek. 20:59. D. 21, '42. Formula's test.

Newsweek. 21:56+. F. 8, '43. Little Steel formula swaying in labor's storm for raises.

Newsweek. 21:62. Mr. 8, '43. Coming crisis in Washington. Ralph Robey.

*Opinion and Comment. 5:1-10. F. 16, '43. First year of price control: an evaluation. J. F. Bell.

Personnel Journal. 21:295-6. F. '43. English wage policy. R. E. Jefferson.

Quarterly Review of Commerce (London). 9, no. 2:75-88. '42. Fight against inflation in total war. Antonin Basch.

Railway Age. 113:572-3. O. 10, '42. President orders wage stabilization.

Review of Economic Statistics. 24:101-13. Ag. '42. What it takes to block inflation. Albert Gailord Hart.

*Rotarian. 60:16-17+. Ja. '42. Ceilings on wages? Yes. Edward A. O'Neal.

*Rotarian. 60:17+. Ja. '42. Ceilings on wages? No. William Green.

Round Table (London). 33:17-23. D. '42. Wages and prices; responsibilities of the government.

Scholastic. 42:6-8. F. '43. Anti-inflation program under attack; demands of farm and labor groups may cause sharp advances in cost of living.

*Science and Society. 7:52-5. Winter, '43. Comments on inflation. Lyle Dowling.

Science and Society. 7:80-7. Winter, '43. National War Labor Board: an achievement in tri-partite administration. Jesse Friedin.

*Southern Economic Journal. 8:504-12. Ap. '42. Wage policy in the defense program. E. B. McNatt.

*Southern Economic Journal. 9:24-32. Jl. '42. General wage ceiling. James J. O'Leary.

*Survey Graphic. 31:85-6. F. '42. Wages and prices in all-out war; reply to I. Lubin. John M. Clark.

*Taxes. 21:75-6+. F. '43. Inflation and low income groups. Jerome R. Hellerstein.

Time. 39:16. My. 11, '42. Chilled but not frozen.

Time. 40:73-4+. Jl. 13, '42. Big battle of Little Steel.

Time. 40:12. Jl. 27, '42. Unstabilized wages.

Time. 40:69. Ag. 17, '42. End of appeasement.

Town Meeting (Bulletin of America's Town Meeting of the Air). 8: 3-18. Je. 25, '42. Wages, taxes, and inflation. Chester Davis, Clinton Davidson, Neil H. Jacoby and Walter Reuther.

Trusts and Estates. 74:351-5. Ap. '42. Road to rationing; results of price and wage control as shown by French experience. Roger Picard.

Trusts and Estates. 75:216-17. S. '42. Farm price and wage inflation.

Trusts and Estates. 75:333-4. O. '42. Inflation battlefront.

Trusts and Estates. 76:67-8. Ja. '43. Wage and salary stabilization; a quiz.

Trusts and Estates. 76:103-4. F. '43. Subsidies or higher prices?

United States News. 12:30, 28. My. 15, 22, '42. Should wage levels be established by Congress or by negotiation conducted by War Labor Board? cross section of opinion.

United States News. 13:24-5. Jl. 24, '42. Our new wage policy; meaning of government's decision to permit increases in steel plants.

United States News. 13:16-17. Jl. 31, '42. Inflation: the facts behind new warnings.

United States News. 14:15-16. F. 19, '43. Showdown on inflation: test for Mr. Byrnes.

United States News. 14:36-8. F. 19, '43. New work week: how rule affects wage disputes.

United States News. 14:28-9. Mr. 19, '43. Inside of a labor dispute; why workers strike in exasperation over confusing tactics of government agencies; difficulties and perplexities of wage stabilization. Paul R. Porter.

United States News. 14:32+. Mr. 19, '43. New troubles for the WLB: wage inconsistency charged.

United States News. 14:20. Mr. 26, '43. John L. Lewis's new challenge; demand for miners' pay rise creates dilemma for administration.

University of Chicago Round Table. No. 200:1-25. Ja. 11, '42. How to meet the menace of inflation. J. M. Clark, T. O. Yntema, and the Roving Reporter.

University of Chicago Round Table. No. 234:1-27. S. 6, '42. Wage policy in wartime. James Carey, Neil Jacoby, and Raleigh Stone.

Vital Speeches of the Day. 8:619-21. Ag. 1, '42. Inflation and its consequences; people not industry will pay for wage increases; radio address, July 9, 1942. Walter D. Fuller.

Vital Speeches of the Day. 9:304-7. Mr. 1, '43. Next steps against inflation; wages and prices must be controlled. James F. Byrnes.

Yale Review. 31, no. 4:684-702. [Je.] '42. Inflation: menace or bogie? Jacob Viner.

...Y DEBATERS' ANNUALS

...IELPS, ED. *Cloth. Price* $2.25

...year books, each a collection of representative intercollegiate debates on important questions of the day. Constructive and rebuttal speeches for both sides. Each debate is accompanied by selected bibliography and briefs.

Vol. XXVIII. 1941-1942.
Federal I... A League... ing; Failu... Needs; A... Based on ... ciples; A Federal ... sory Saving; Post-War ... Western Hemisphere Solidarity; ... dom of Speech in Time of National Emergency.

Vol. XXVII. 1940-1941.
Industry Can Solve the Employment Problem; Conscription of Capital for Defense; Preservation of Democracy Through Decreased Government Control; Interstate Trade Barriers; Japanese Aggression; Union of United States and British Commonwealth of Nations; Regulation of the American Press; Compulsory Military Training; Strikes in Defense Industries; Western Hemisphere Defense.

Vol. XXVI. 1939-1940.
The Basis of a Lasting Peace; Shall the United States Enter the War?; Government Ownership and Operation of Railroads; Neutrality of the United States; Extension of Reciprocal Trade Agreements; The Third Term for President; Should the Roosevelt Administration Be Approved?; The Dies Committee; Civil Liberties; Labor; Foreign Affairs; Government and Business.

Vol. XXV. 1938-1939.
The Increase in the National Debt; The Anglo-American Alliance; Government Ownership and Operation of the Railroads; Alliance of United States, France and Great Britain Against Fascism; Have the Achievements of Science Brought Progress?; American Solidarity; The Problem of Unemployment; The American Newspaper; "Pump-priming" Should Cease; Government and Health.

Vol. XXIV. 1937-1938.
... Prosperity; ...uropean Af... States Citi... ademic Free... ts Subversive ... ucation; Amer... s; Anglo-American ... Pact; N.L.R.A. and ... of Industrial Disputes; Unicameral Legislatures; Uniform Marriage Laws; Regulation of Advertising.

Vol. XXIII. 1936-1937.
The Constitution a Menace; Government Ownership of Electric Utilities; Subsidizing College Athletes; Teachers' Oaths; Unicameral Legislatures; Economic Internationalism; Minimum Wages and Maximum Hours (two debates); Consumers' Cooperatives; The Present-day Family as a Social Institution; The Sit-down Strike.

Vol. XXII. 1935-1936.
A Written Constitution a Hindrance to Social Progress; State Medicine; Compulsory Military Training; Legalization of Sweepstakes; Admission of Negroes to State Universities; The Neutrality Policy of the United States; The Parole System; Admission of Hawaii as a State; Limitation of the Power of the Supreme Court (two debates).

Vol. XXI. 1934-1935.
Equalizing Educational Opportunity; An Evaluation of the New Deal; Social Services and Unemployment Relief; International Traffic in Arms and Munitions; Democratic Collectivism; The Agricultural Adjustment Administration; Collective Bargaining; Government Ownership and Operation of Public Utilities; Pacifism the Highest Form of Patriotism; Japan and Naval Parity.

Vols. XII-XX. available. Contents furnished on request.